Sea Salt Sweet

THE ART OF USING SALTS FOR
THE ULTIMATE DESSERT EXPERIENCE

❧ HEATHER BAIRD ❧

RUNNING PRESS
PHILADELPHIA · LONDON

Books published by Running Press are available at special discounts for bulk
purchases in the United States by corporations, institutions, and other organizations.
For more information, please contact the Special Markets Department at the Perseus
Books Group, 2300 Chestnut Street, Suite 200, Philadelphia, PA 19103, or call
(800) 810-4145, ext. 5000, or e-mail special.markets@perseusbooks.com.

ISBN 978-0-7624-5396-2
Library of Congress Control Number: 2015942586

E-book ISBN 978-0-7624-5811-0

9 8 7 6 5 4 3 2 1
Digit on the right indicates the number of this printing

Cover and interior design by Susan Van Horn
Edited by Jennifer Kasius
Typography: Archer, Beton, Isabella Script, Museo, Neutra Text and Nymphette

Running Press Book Publishers
2300 Chestnut Street
Philadelphia, PA 19103-4371

Visit us on the web!
www.offthemenublog.com
www.sprinklebakes.com

I dedicate this book to my
grandmother Rosa Finley.
Your spirit is with me always.

∽ contents ∽

acknowledgments

THANKS TO MY SUPPORTIVE AGENT Lindsay Edgecombe. I'm so glad to know you. To Kristen Wiewora, thank you for being the champion of this book. Thank you to Jennifer Kasius for your marvelous editing. To Frances Soo Ping Chow and Susan Van Horn, thank you for your masterful design work. Personal thanks to the spirit of Rosa Finley, who is likely the chief biscuit maker of Heaven, and to the spirit of Clark Crutchfield for peanuts and Coca-Cola.

To my husband, Mark, who is thoughtful with his criticism, and makes the best rocket fuel coffee this side of the Mason-Dixon, thank you with the utmost sincerity. My mother, Katie Watts, and her right-hand man, Larry Watts, yes absolutely without question, they are the most dependable people I know. Words could never express enough gratitude to the two of you.

Thanks to Megan Charette for sharing her many talents, including recipe testing and metric conversions. Cheers to Ann Nelson with Merlot and doughnuts. Thank you, Christen Blackman Ferrer, for always giving me the center piece of cake. Heartfelt thanks to Heather Radecky for her unwavering support and especially her fine recipe testing and opinions. Sincere thanks to Heather Alexander for words over brunch and encouragement and advice. Thanks to the wonderful artist and baker Michael Willen for allowing me to peer through his eyes at my own recipes.

From the bottom of my heart I thank the people who have generously allowed me to explore new ideas in baking with new audiences: Meghan McAndrews at Betty Crocker, editors Aleksa Brown and Alison Feldman of *The Etsy Blog*, Kenzie Kramer and Sarah Martens at *Better Homes and Gardens*.

Thanks to the food bloggers who inspire me with their incredible talents, especially Darla Wireman, Sue Sparks, Tina Chambers, Megan DeKok, Kristan Roland, Shelly Jaronsky, the two Pauls behind *Sweet Paul Magazine*: Paul Lowe and Paul Vitale, Rosie Alyea, and Shauna Sever.

Never last, my deepest gratitude to all the readers and supporters of *Sprinkle Bakes*.

introduction

I KNOW JUST WHERE IT ALL STARTED, the love I have for salty and sweet together. It began with a special snack that my dad and I shared when I was a kid. I'd often ride to the gas station with him in his old beat-up work truck. While he filled the tank, I'd go inside the mini mart with a few dollars he'd given me to get our favorite snack. This was a couple of colas and two sleeves of salted peanuts. Back then twist-off bottle caps were a rarity, so the cashier would pop the tops with the bottle opener mounted behind the counter.

Once back in the truck, our ritual began. A couple of swigs were taken to make room for the peanuts, and then the entire two-ounce bag was funneled into the mouth of the bottle. And finally, the all-important last step—an extra tap-tap-tap on the end of the upright-turned bag to make sure all the salt made it into the soda. There was something about the saltiness of the peanuts that made the cola taste even sweeter. There we'd sit in comfortable silence, sipping cola and crunching peanuts, our view through the dirty windshield somehow improved.

I'm pretty sure the peanut and cola combo is only known south of the Mason-Dixon Line, but it's documented in an old country song sang by Barbara Mandrell that describes her not wanting to seem like too much of a "hayseed" and slipping peanuts into her Coke when no one was looking. As a kid I never knew that I should be ashamed of the love I had for my favorite salty-sweet snack; I just knew that it tasted good. It seems that we were on to something back then. Salty sweets are embraced in many cultures and now they're on menus in trendy restaurants, too.

To me, salty and sweet together is the ultimate flavor combination. If you've ever dipped pretzels in melted chocolate or sprinkled salt over a juicy melon slice, then I suspect you feel the same way. The magic is simple. Salt stimulates the appetite, while sweetness satiates it. When the two come together in just the right amounts and with the right other ingredients, they stimulate a multitude of taste buds all at once—and that's seriously exciting news for your palate! When salt is used judiciously on dessert, it is alchemized into something deliciously complex and rewarding. Candy caramels with fleur de sel are infinitely more satisfying than something that's just sweet. Don't get me wrong—I love sweet (sweet is my life!) but my favorite desserts always have a counter or foil against one-dimensional sweet.

Today, as an avid baker with a vocal community of bakers on my blog Sprinkle Bakes, I can say that salty sweets garner some of the most comments and enthusiasm among the desserts I post. My favorite pastime is thinking up new ways to incorporate sea salt into dessert, and there's a wealth of inspiration and flavors to draw from. Chocolate and caramel are perhaps the most obvious and well-loved flavors to marry with salt (and for good reason). Munchable salty kettle-cooked chips and pretzels can be added to cookie dough and candies to marvelous effect. Salt tempers bitterness in tart berries and makes the sweetness in citrus fruits shine. And perhaps less obvious are such ingredients as cheese, olives, and red wine, which all contain delicious savory notes known as umami and are wonderful components to use in the salty-sweet kitchen (be sure to read more about umami on page 170). The possibilities are endless, really.

salt savvy

EVERY KIND OF SALT IN THE ENTIRE world comes from a deposit that is created when salt water evaporates. Whether it is from a modern ocean or a saltwater lake (such as the Dead Sea), or even from an ancient underground sea, all salt is sea salt; however, not all salts are the same.

Salt comes in many forms, and to use it properly in cooking and baking you must familiarize yourself with it. You should know how it tastes and how it feels when pinched between your fingers. You need to become salt savvy, and unless you are best friends with a selmelier (that means salt expert), it can be difficult to understand how vastly salts differ.

Here's some more information on common types of salt:

Table salt: The most common salt is sodium chloride, or table salt, and it is made up of the elements sodium and chlorine (NaCl). We've established that all salt is sea salt, but whatever mineral and flavor nuances the ocean gives to salt, they are stripped away in a factory to create man-made table salt: stark white and uniform in grain. The salt used to make table salt is typically mined from the earth before it is industrially refined. When it reaches grocery store shelves, it can contain up to 99.9 percent sodium chloride; the remaining percentage is made up of anticaking agents and iodine. Iodine was first added to table salt by the US government in the 1920s, when there was a high incidence of thyroid disease due to iodine deficiency. It remains in salt as a preventative measure today, although most of us get enough iodine from eating seafood, greens, and dairy.

Sea salt: Sea salt is a generic term for unrefined salt that is harvested from a modern ocean or saltwater deposit, and contains inherent trace minerals from its environment. These residual minerals give sea salts their unique flavors and colors. Many sea salts are artisan salts, which means the salt is hand harvested by a skilled craftsperson, rather than being manufactured at a salt plant. Sea salt is widely varied in characteristics. It comes in flake and granular forms; it is milled in coarse chunks or ground fine; it can be damp with sea water or made dry by evaporation or due to its mineral content, and it varies in weight and color.

Kosher salt: Kosher salt is manufactured by compacting granular salt, which produces large, irregular, platelike, hollow shapes. Like table salt, kosher salt consists of sodium chloride (NaCl), but because of its unique shape, it weighs less than table salt. Kosher salt typically does not contain iodine or anticaking agents, so it has a clean, light flavor. Many chefs love to cook with this salt because it adheres well to food and dissolves easily. Kosher salt is so named because of its use in treating meats to make them kosher.

Rock salt: Also called "earth salt," rock salt is mined from underground. It originates from deposits left over from ancient bodies of water that were cut off from the oceans millions of years ago. When the water evaporated, salt was left on Earth's surface. As ages of sediments covered the salt deposits, weight and pressure compressed the salt into rock layers. These layers are hundreds of feet below today's ground surface, or embedded in mountains. Mined rock salt is commonly used to make table salt, and in a coarser, less-refined form it is used in ice-cream makers and to deice roads.

a rainbow of sea salts

OVER THE PAST COUPLE OF YEARS I've experimented with many different salts in my baking, and my favorites tend to be those that have never seen the inside of an industrial processing plant. The salts I reach for most often are the hand-harvested varieties that retain flavor and color subtleties from the bodies of water from whence they came. These salts are what we generally refer to as "sea salt" today, although some may come from underground and not directly from a coastline. Not only are these artisan sea salts tasty and beautiful, but some of my fondest memories are from trips to the ocean, so it feels special when I use sea salts in my baking. It's like bringing a little piece of the ocean into your life and dessert.

Sea salt comes in all different colors: pink, red, black, blue, and everything in between—and where there's color, there's flavor, too. Some salts get their colors from minerals in their environment and others from infusion processes, such as smoking or hand blending. As previously stated, these salts can be sourced from most anywhere—from modern oceans or salt lakes, or mined from the earth.

For example, pink rock salt gets its color from minerals in the earth, but another type of pink salt found in salt lakes gets a rosy hue from a microbe called Halobacteria, which produces a red carotenoid pigment similar to that found in tomatoes. Hawaiian red alaea salt gets its red-rust color from iron-rich volcanic clay. Black lava salt is a salt harvested from a modern ocean and hand blended with activated charcoal, giving it a smoky black color.

The myriad of colorful sea salts available today weren't always a chef's sought-after prize. Old-time salt producers called these "dirty salts" and would strive to make salt white and uniform in grain. The "dirt" these critics referred to is an elemental factor from the salt's natural environment, such as the many trace minerals that makes sel gris, well, *gris* (French for "gray").

Whether it was a change of mind or heart, today, the prejudices of early detractors are all but forgotten. Now we celebrate salt with its many flavors and colors. New (and old) sea salts of every culture, climate, and geography are more procurable than ever. They are becoming unhidden from their cultural niches; so much that we are now able to intimately connect a singular salt to the person who made it. It's a way of tasting the world: from the immaculate shores surrounding the island of Molokai in Hawaii to England's low-lying marshlands of Maldon. Salt has the power to transport you.

baking with salt and sodium intake

SEA SALT HAS ALWAYS BEEN A CRUCIAL element in baking. In addition to contributing to the overall flavor of confections, it serves a chemical function. In many of these recipes it's used as a leavening agent. In bread baking, it controls the fermentation rate of yeast and it has a strengthening effect on the gluten protein in dough. It also promotes browning. It's the unseen ingredient in the "A Pinch" chapter, and as chapters progress to "Well-Seasoned," salt becomes more prominent—visible, even. You'll spot as a garnish on cakes and pastries.

But there's one thing I should make crystal clear. Salt should always be used mindfully, because desserts with overt salt flavor usually do not taste good. The recipes in this book strive for balance, and if salt is more pronounced in a dish it's because of how it's used, and not because we're just heaping salt on top of a cupcake.

Sodium is a nutrient vital to human life. It is an electrolyte that keeps our cells, muscles, and nervous system working. It regulates the balance of water in the body, helps control muscle contractions, and maintains normal heart rhythm. That being said, medical studies have linked high salt consumption to such health complications as cardiovascular disease and stroke. Too much salt is bad for you.

The biggest contributor to our sodium consumption is not the salt we add to food at home. It's hidden in processed foods and lots of other unsalty-tasting products. About 75 percent of the sodium we eat comes from processed foods and restaurant foods. The Centers for Disease Control and Prevention recommends consuming less than 2,300 milligrams of sodium per day (about 1 teaspoon of table salt). This reminds us that we must use salt mindfully, and with purpose.

Because salt is already added to some of the food we buy, I recommend becoming a label reader. If you are buying or preparing food for someone for whom high blood pressure, diabetes, obesity, or heart disease is an issue, then strict salt-watching is recommended for good health.

gourmet and artisan sea salts

THERE ARE CERTAIN CHARACTERISTICS to keep in mind when selecting sea salts to use in dessert. Coarse salts have staying power, which means they melt slowly, so they are best employed as finishing salts (that means you sprinkle them on top of the dessert after plating). And there are other virtues to consider, such as the intense smoky aroma of alderwood-smoked salt and the charcoal aesthetic of Hawaiian black lava salt. There's a whole world of sea salts to choose from and that can be overwhelming, so I've got a great short list to get you started. Purchase a few salts highlighted in this section, and then add more exotic salts to your collection as your interest grows. I offer few guidelines for using these salts in dessert, but no strict rules. At first, try to follow my recommendations for the textures of salt used in each recipe, and after you get a feel for how coarse salt crunches and velvet salt melts instantly—experiment! Be playful and creative. Don't be afraid to swap out Hawaiian red alaea salt for fleur de sel; just try it and see what happens.

Most of the recipes in this book use the salts listed in this section, and although they sound exotic, you may able to find many of them locally. To my surprise and delight, I've seen fleur de sel and Hawaiian red alaea salt at my local small-town grocery store. But if you're coming up empty handed, nearly any specialty sea salt can be procured via the World Wide Web. Refer to the "Online Resources and Suppliers" section (page 228) for good sources.

Fleur de sel (flower of salt): This slightly coarse, moist, and mineral-tasting salt is considered the finest of all sea salts, and it's my personal favorite. It has a high mineral content, and the residuals give it a light gray to pink color. It is lauded by professional chefs, and is primarily used as a finishing salt.

Most French fleur de sel is hand harvested off the coast of Brittany, in the town of Guérande. The salt is also produced in quantity in Portugal; similar to its French cousin, it is called flôr de sal. These salt crystals are hand harvested from the top layer of salt marshes by salt workers (paludiers) who skim the water's surface with a wooden rake. This tool picks up the purest flakes and leaves the heavy sel gris (gray salt) in the lower levels of the salt marshes. This type of salt harvesting started all the way back in the ninth century, and at the time, only women were allowed to collect the flakes; men were deemed too heavy handed for the delicate task. This harvesting method has remained largely unchanged over the centuries, except now male paludiers are also allowed to participate in harvesting.

Due to the labor-intensive production of making this salt, it costs more than traditional sea salt, but at around $10 for 4 ounces, it's not a prohibitively expensive way to enhance your confectionery. You can usually find an inexpensive pinch tin if you're looking to experiment with it before committing to a larger supply. I use it on everything from vanilla ice cream to chocolate truffles, and I can't make a batch of shortbread without a sprinkle before baking.

Maldon sea salt: This clean-tasting, brittle, pyramid-shaped flake salt is harvested on England's south coast. Certain environmental elements, such as low rainfall and a high wind, help produce good salty water in its birthplace, the low-lying marshlands of Maldon. This sea water is filtered and boiled to remove impurities, and then heated until the salt crystalizes. The result is an additive-free, clean-tasting salt with the benefits of such trace

minerals as magnesium and calcium. Refer to the flake salt entry (page 20) for a more complete description of the texture of flake salt. Although it has many uses, it is primarily a finishing salt. I particularly love sprinkling it on brownies and other gooey bar recipes. I am additionally fond of a smoked variety of Maldon salt. It's cold-smoked, which means the flakes are exposed to smoke but not to heat, so it retains its delicate shape. The flavor of the salt is unique to the hardwoods used as firewood in the smoking process. I especially like to add this smoked version to the Milk Caramel Pops (page 120), or any caramel, for that matter.

Hawaiian red alaea salt: This red salt is hugely rich in minerals and has a clean, mellow flavor that lingers on the tongue. It is harvested in natural volcanic-baked red clay called alaea. Its coarse texture and bright color makes it ideal for finishing. Depending on the harvest, the color can range from light pink to orange-red to deep red. Traditionally, Hawaiians have been using this salt in cleansing ceremonies and for healing and medicinal purposes, and it's a traditional seasoning for native Hawaiian dishes. I love pairing it with chocolate. A sprinkling atop chocolate bark or even on chocolate chip cookies adds a whole new level of flavor and eye appeal to these sweets.

Hawaiian black lava salt: This salt has a mild, unbitter flavor and it is usually harvested from the pristine waters surrounding the island of Molokai in Hawaii. It is rich in trace minerals and gets its obsidian color from activated charcoal. The charcoal is added after harvesting and will smudge onto fingers when pinched, so it's a good idea to have a towel handy for cleanup. You can usually find it in coarse crystals, and due to its beauty and texture it makes a great finishing salt. Try it on ice cream or my favorite, Watermelon Granita (page 117).

Alderwood-smoked salt: This salt has a distinctive rich flavor and a well-pronounced (some would say aggressive) smoky scent that will waft out of the open container. The smoking method used to give this salt its unique flavor is centuries old, and involves placing sea salt above a burning alderwood fire. It is sold as fine-grain or coarse crystals, so it can be added during cooking or used as a finishing salt. Use it to give desserts an obvious smoky flavor. It goes well with such warm flavors as cinnamon and bourbon. I sometimes use a sprinkling over slices of Bourbon Brown Sugar Pound Cake (page 70).

Sel gris: *Sel gris* means "gray salt" in French, but it's also known as Celtic sea salt. It is born from the same method as fleur de sel, but instead of being raked off the top of the water; the salt is allowed to come into contact with the lower salt-crystallizing pan. This gives the salt mineral complexity and a gray color. The flavor is briny and tastes of the ocean water from which it was harvested, so it works well with other assertive flavors, such as tart berries and lemon. It is damp and coarse, and an excellent choice for using in homemade salt blends (see "Salt Blends," page 218). It is also available in a drier form for use in grinders, and yet another version called "velvet" sea salt is highly pulverized and almost flourlike in consistency.

Himalayan block sea salt: These luminescent pink blocks lend a kiss of salt to anything that comes in contact with their surfaces. The salt blocks are mined from deep deposits formed from the remains of a great inland ocean, and today, they are excavated from those deposits in large sheets. Salt blocks have many virtues, and for a more complete picture of them I recommend reading *Salt Block Cooking*, a book by Mark Bitterman, selmelier and owner of The Meadow salts shops in Portland, Oregon, and in New York.

salt textures

THERE ARE MANY THINGS TO LEARN about sea salt before adding it to a recipe, from the minutiae of mineral flavors to the geographic birthplaces and everything in between, but perhaps the most important consideration is texture. Understanding the difference between grains, crystals, and flakes will best help you use them in your confectionery. You'll know exactly when and where to add salt (into the batter versus a sprinkling on top) and that will make a world of difference in a finished dish.

The salts will fall under one of four categories: fine grain, coarse, flake, and velvet. Block salt also gets an honorable mention here, but as the name indicates, it's a solid sheet of salt (usually mined 4 x 8 x 2 inches/10 x 20 x 5 cm and larger) and it is used as a surface on which to prepare and serve food.

Fine grain: This is often referred to as "cooking salt." I keep a salt cellar of fine grain in my kitchen because it is so versatile. It goes in almost everything I make because it can be substituted in equal amounts for table salt. It is used in the recipes throughout this book and is a must-have for the "A Pinch" chapter. It melts easily and works well in batter, dough, sauces—you name it! Fine-grain sea salt is widely available, though most any coarse-grain sea salt can be ground fine in a mill or mortar and pestle.

Coarse: Large crystals and granules are best used as finishing salts because they melt slowly. They linger on the tongue and crunch between the teeth. This means you'll get a burst of intense salinity when you bite into a hefty piece, so in general, it should be used sparingly. Some coarse varieties are dry, and therefore a good choice to use in a grinder. Other granules are damp—you can feel the moisture with a finger pinch and taste the sea water from which it was harvested.

Flake: Flake salts are largely used as finishing salt due to their beautiful shape and delicate crunch, but they can easily be added as an ingredient in cooking and baking.

The crystals are harvested into thin pyramid shapes and this creates a brittle flake that is easily crushed between the fingers. In general its flavor is clean and clear: a single fleeting note that contains no bitterness. You can also find flake with flavor complexities, such as smoked and herb-infused. The large crystals look striking on desserts, especially on a dark background of chocolate ganache, and hold their shape well. Some flake salts dissolve easier than others. Maldon flake salt is a sturdy variety that has more staying power and can be used on juicy fruits and other moist surfaces.

Extra fine: This texture is sometimes referred to as velvet. The salt, usually sel gris, is ground to a fine flour and it can be used in cooking and baking, and as a finishing salt. It melts instantly on a moist surface, and it does a good job of clinging to popcorn and other dry foods. Due to its fine nature, a little goes a long way, so be sure to use a judicious hand when adding it to a recipe.

Block salt: Salt blocks come in a variety of shapes and sizes and can be used in cooking because they conduct heat, but for our purposes, these blocks are chilled to keep food cold for an extended period of time or used at room temperature as a serving tray. When juicy fruits and berries are placed on these blocks, they break down and take on clean, gentle salinity. Chocolate can be poured directly on the cold salt slab to make the most crave-worthy chocolate curls you've ever had. Take proper care of your salt block, and it will be your kitchen ally for years to come. They are naturally antimicrobial, so cleanup is easy. Just run the block under a stream of water and wipe it gently. Repeated use will cause the salt block to diminish in size over time, and when it becomes too small to utilize for cooking or chilling, simply break it into small coarse pieces with a kitchen-dedicated mallet for use in a salt grinder.

salty language
(a glossary)

WHAT'S THE DIFFERENCE BETWEEN COOKING SALT AND GRINDER SALT? What makes artisan salt so special? Salt has its own language, and several terms can all mean the same thing, so you may find yourself scratching your head in the grocery store aisle. This quick reference will help you decipher the lingo, and will define many of the words you may see on manufacturer's labels while procuring salts for use at home.

Artisan salt: A salt that is produced more extensively than by just the evaporation of sea water. This can refer to smoked salts and sea salts that are created in solar houses, rather than evaporated naturally outdoors. Maldon smoked salt is a good example of an artisan sea salt.

Bay salt: Another word for sea salt.

Blended/flavored sea salt: Any sea salt blended with herbs, spices, citrus, or other flavorings. These blends can be made in small batches at home (see page 218) and are used primarily as finishing salts.

Celtic sea salt: A gray French sea salt. This salt is also referred to as sel gris.

Cooking salt: Sea salt that is fine grain so that it dissolves easily during cooking.

Earth salt: Salt that is mined from the earth. Himalayan salt blocks are an example of mined sea salts.

Finishing salt: Any salt, although usually coarse or flake texture, used to season a dish after it is cooked, assembled or plated.

Fumée de sel: Smoked sea salt.

Grinder salt: Any large, usually dry crystal sea salt suitable for a salt mill or grinder.

Hand harvested: Salt harvested by man in small batches. It can be evaporated in ponds or salt pans from any body of water or evaporated in salt tanks. Hand-harvested salts are also called artisan salts because they are more extensively produced.

Iodized salt: A table salt fortified with a small amount of iodine during processing.

Kosher salt: A coarse-grain salt whose grains have been compressed, creating a flat flake rather than granule shape, which has a lighter weight that sticks better to food. Most kosher salt sold is not sea salt.

Natural salt: Made from salt water that has been solar evaporated in salt pans by sun and high winds. Harvesting takes place once the water has evaporated, and it is crushed and ground as needed without further refining.

Popcorn salt: Another term for velvet salt. It's a very fine-grain salt that sticks better to popcorn and other dry foods.

Rock salt: Also known as ice-cream salt. This is the least refined salt and is not suitable for consumption. It is used for reducing the freezing point of ice for ice-cream makers.

Salt evaporation ponds: These are also called salterns or salt pans, and are shallow artificial ponds designed to extract salts from sea water or other brines.

Saunier: A salt worker or salt seller. *Saunier* refers to anyone who works in the salt industry.

Selmelier: Refers to a trained and knowledgeable professional specializing in salt and its culinary uses. This word was coined by food writer and salt guru Mark Bitterman.

Table salt: Mechanically mined, refined salt with undesirable anticaking additives.

Traditional sea salt: This is an umbrella term for dry, coarse sea salts that come from various geographic locations. These salts are unrefined, usually hand harvested and solar evaporated. These are often used as grinder salts and can be milled to a desired texture.

getting started

MAYBE YOU'VE HEARD THAT OLD fortune cookie wisdom "Failing to plan is planning to fail." I've often cracked open a cookie to find that fortune, and as someone who loves spontaneity, I find it a little stinging (who writes those fortunes, anyway?). But truly, it is sound advice. It's good to have a strategy before embarking on any project, and I always try to apply this to my baking endeavors. Following are rules I practice to make the most of my time in the kitchen. It helps me to focus and have full presence of mind for the task at hand.

Mise en place: This French phrase means "set up" or "everything in place." It means to have all your ingredients prepared before you start mixing and baking. Nuts and chocolate can be chopped ahead of time; pans can be lined with parchment paper and ready to receive freshly mixed batter. Doing a little prep before you start can greatly reduce stress when it comes time to put everything together. There'll be no last-minute running to the store for a missing ingredient, or rummaging through tool drawers for a candy thermometer. Nearly every cookbook on my shelf suggests this baking procedure, and it bears repeating. "Everything in place" makes your time in the kitchen more enjoyable and your end result more successful.

Read the recipe: It's a smart thing to do. Give it a good once-over from beginning to end. This may seem like common sense, but I've been guilty of jumping head first into a seemingly straightforward pudding recipe that later required a sieve through cheesecloth, and that's not something I always have on hand.

Measuring: You'll notice that all the recipes in this book use both volume and weight measurements, and of the two, weight measurements are the more precise. Digital scales are widely available, inexpensive, and easy to use, so why not get one? While it's true that

weighing ingredients is all about accuracy, it's also about efficiency. When the scale is set at zero, an ingredient can be placed on the scale until it reaches the suggested amount. You can then weigh one ingredient after another in the same bowl just by zeroing your scale (labeled as "tare" function on the device) after each addition. I especially love that it reduces the amount of dishes I have to clean.

Cup measurements can drastically vary depending on how tightly you pack dry ingredients, such as flour, into the cup. If you don't have a scale, spoon flour into a dry measuring cup until overflowing, then level the mixture with a long metal spatula or the back of a straight knife. Avoid scooping from the flour container; doing so can cause the flour to become compressed in the cup and the baked goods will be dense.

Large glass measures are used for liquid ingredients, and they have a spout for easy pouring. The best way to measure liquid ingredients in a large glass cup is to place the cup on a flat surface at eye level.

Baking: When you turn the oven dial to 350°F/180°C and expect it to heat to the precise temperature, keep your fingers crossed. It's a wish. Just because the oven beeps and flashes 350°F/180°C does not mean that's what's going on inside the oven. Unfortunately, it's common for ovens to be inaccurate; some have hot spots and some heat slowly. Oven thermometers are the remedy to this problem. They hang right inside the oven and gauge the actual surrounding temperature, so you can adjust your oven dial to compensate and have a more accurate bake time. You can buy them inexpensively at kitchen specialty stores and online.

Blooming gelatin: Unflavored gelatin is "bloomed" in liquid before being added as an ingredient to many desserts. To bloom gelatin, sprinkle it evenly over liquid as the recipe indicates and let stand for 3 to 5 minutes. Avoid dumping the powder in all at once; this can cause lumps to form and the gelatin will not absorb evenly. Well-bloomed gelatin will form a semitranslucent solid mass. When it is heated, it dissolves evenly as it becomes liquid, and can be added to custards, mousses, and similar smooth-textured desserts.

Folding batter: Meringue and whipped cream are often combined with other ingredients to create a fluffy texture in desserts. Use this folding technique to avoid deflating the ingredients as you mix them together.

Place the ingredients in a bowl as directed by the recipe, and grab a large rubber spatula. Cut through the middle of the ingredients with the thin edge of the spatula in a straight line. With a scooping motion, scrape the bottom of the bowl and turn the ingredients over with the spatula as you bring it up to the surface. Turn the bowl counterclockwise (toward yourself) with your free hand as you do this. Repeat the folding method until the ingredients are well incorporated.

Proofing yeast: Stale active dry yeast is a baking disaster just waiting to happen. If you've had yeast on hand for a while and you're not sure if it's still fresh, there's an easy way to check it. In a 1-cup/240 ml measure, dissolve 1 teaspoon of granulated sugar in ½ cup/60 ml of warm tap water heated to 110°F to 115°F/40° to 45°C. If you don't have a thermometer, the tap water should be warm but not hot to the touch. Stir in 2¼ teaspoons (1 [¼-ounce/7 g] package) of room-temperature active dry yeast until there are no more dry yeast granules on the surface. In 3 to 4 minutes, the yeast should start to rise. After 10 minutes, the yeast mixture should be very foamy and should have risen to the top of the 1-cup/120 ml measure. If the mixture doesn't foam and rise, then it's time to buy new active dry yeast.

Cooling: This is in an important step that should never be skipped (okay, such emergencies as midnight chocolate chip cookies excluded, and if you don't mind burned fingers). Most cakes should be completely cool before frosting goes on; cookies will fall apart if removed too soon from the baking sheet. Muffins and quick breads should be removed from their pan soon after baking and transferred to cooling racks or they will sweat on the bottom, and that produces a soggy texture and promotes bacterial growth.

baking equipment

SUCCESSFUL BAKING RELIES ON GOOD TOOLS AS MUCH AS IT DOES on techniques and ingredients. Seasoned home bakers will have most of the cooking equipment listed here, and beginner bakers can use this as a guide to growing their bakeware arsenal. Most of the equipment used in this book can be found here, but if a recipe uses something that isn't on this list, it is usually mentioned at the beginning of the recipe.

These are essentials I just can't live without!

Bowls: Graduated (or nesting) heatproof bowls are essential to every baker. They are ideal for a variety of uses and will store easily. I find a set of glass bowls and a set of stainless-steel bowls will cover nearly every kitchen task.

Cake pans: I use aluminum 8- and 9-inch/20 and 23 cm round pans with 2-inch/5 cm-deep sides most often. Straight-sided cake pans make for beautiful, professional-looking cakes, and they make layering easy, too.

Candy thermometer: Candy thermometers determine the various stages (soft ball to hard crack) of boiled candies. Because accuracy is so important with candy making, it's a good idea to calibrate your thermometer before using it. You don't have to do this every time you use it, but periodically checking it can help prevent some sad surprises. Here's how.

Insert the candy thermometer into a pot of water and bring the water to a vigorous boil. Allow the thermometer to stand in the water for several minutes before checking the temperature. If it reads 212°F/100°C, your thermometer is accurate. If not, take into account the temperature difference with all your future cooking. If your thermometer is more than a few degrees off or gives you drastically different results from your calibrations, it's time to get a new thermometer.

Coffee or spice grinder: I use a small electric coffee bean grinder to make homemade salt blends (see page 218). Because coffee is so aromatic, I have a dedicated machine just for making blended salts. It's the most efficient tool for the job since it takes only two to four pulses to blend the salt and inclusions together. Most grinders are inexpensive and are easily found at discount stores.

Cookie cutters: If you're like me, you have too many, but if you're the conservative sort, a standard set of graduated round cutters will handle most cookie-cutting needs. If you choose metal cutters, rusting can occur after washing, so dry them in the oven at 120°F/49°C to prevent this from happening.

Cooling racks: Cross-wire cooling racks are favorites of mine because they have a tight grid and small desserts, such as mini cakes and bite-size cookies, won't teeter on wires spaced too far apart.

Cupcake or muffin pans: Every baker needs at least one standard-size cupcake pan. Even if you don't like cupcakes (and I know deep down you really do—it's just cake and frosting in a single serving), they can be used to make tarts and individual-size cheesecakes. Aluminum pans are a good choice, but nonstick pans are perhaps easier to clean.

Electric mixers: I collect hand mixers and it's getting to be a real storage problem, so I'll go ahead and say you only need one. Choose a mixer with seven speeds or higher, especially if you're not opting to spring for a standing mixer.

I often use a KitchenAid 5-quart/4.7 L mixer for big jobs, such as making large-batch cookies and kneading yeast breads. The attachments (whisk, paddle, and dough hook) are interchangeable and help tackle any recipe.

Food processor: This tool has become a permanent fixture on my countertop. There's really no equal to its efficiency when it comes to making tart bases and pie crusts. You can also whiz ordinary granulated sugar to extra-fine for meringues, and it makes chopping nuts a snap. For smaller jobs I use an electric mini chopper.

Measuring cups and spoons: Liquid measuring cups are available in 1-, 2-, 4- and 8-cup/240, 480, 960, and 1,900 ml capacities. The 4-cup/960 ml is a good all-purpose size to keep on hand and suits most baking needs. Measuring cups are used for dry ingredients and other foods that can be heaped into a cup, such as flour, sour cream, and vegetable shortening. Stainless-steel cups and spoons are the most useful and durable, in my opinion.

Microwave oven: Most kitchen dwellers can get by without the use of a microwave, but I find it to be an essential tool for a variety of uses. I use it for softening butter, melting and tempering chocolate, and popping popcorn (see Homemade Microwave Popcorn, page 149).

Offset spatulas: These spatulas have a bend right below the handle, and are helpful for loosening cakes from pans. I always use them for applying, spreading, and smoothing frostings onto cakes and other confections.

Parchment and waxed paper: Unbleached, silicone-coated parchment paper is my go-to for cookie sheets because it can be reused several times. I also use it to line cake pans to ensure flawless removal. Waxed paper is great for wrapping soft caramels (such as Ale and Pretzel Soft Caramels, page 133). I often use a small sheet as a resting place for sticky spatulas and spoons during intermittent stirring and folding.

Pastry brushes: Natural boar's hair–bristle pastry brushes are best. Use these for buttering layers of phyllo dough or glazing cakes with simple syrup.

Rubber spatulas: Five or more of these are in regular rotation in my kitchen. They are used for folding meringue and sponge-based cakes, and to efficiently scrape every last bit of batter or icing from bowls and containers. I find mini spatulas very useful for scraping such foods as sour cream or yogurt from small measuring cups.

Salt cellar: A salt cellar is a piece of tableware that holds salt. The containers are produced in a variety of sizes and can be lidded or open. Large salt cellars are referred to as a master salt, because they remain in place, whereas smaller cellars can be passed around a table. In these modern times, cellars have been almost replaced by salt shakers, which is unfortunate, if you ask me. It's difficult to control the amount of salt pouring out of a shaker, and most shakers are made for finer grinds of salt. Cellars make it easy to pinch and scoop the amount of salt needed.

Salt mill or salt grinder: This is a handheld device that is used for grinding salt. Briny, damp salt will cause grinders with metal blades to rust, so use coarse, dry salt in these grinders. Damp salts may be used in grinders with a ceramic blade without the worry of corrosion. I like having a grinder on the table for finishing all kinds of dishes.

Scale: If you're shopping for your first scale (or a new one), I suggest a digital scale with a large, illuminated readout. I use this type of model (purchased for less than $20) and it meets all my measuring needs as a home baker. You'll have to change the batteries eventually, but it's a small price to pay for the convenience and accuracy. The scale is perhaps the most neglected kitchen gadget in the United States, as we usually measure by volume (cups) and not weight. I think we continue to measure this way because it's what we grew up with. We watched our baking mentors (moms, dads, grandmothers) measure with cups, but I feel attitudes are shifting, as American home bakers are discovering the ease and efficiency of using a scale.

Sieves and sifters: Sifters are used to aerate flour and other dry ingredients to create a light, fluffy texture in baked goods. I prefer simple fine-mesh strainers to the tiresome hand-cranked or squeeze-handled variety.

Springform pan: No kitchen arsenal would be complete without a springform pan (or two). I use those with an 8- or 9-inch/20 or 23 cm diameter often. Choose springform pans that are a full 3 inches/4.5 cm deep and labeled as "leakproof."

Whisks: These are available in metal, plastic, and silicone coated. I use the metal variety in various sizes, but my large balloon whisk is well worn from repeated use. It does a great job whisking dry ingredients together and incorporating air into cream.

ingredients

GREAT DESSERTS BEGIN AND END with quality ingredients, and that includes such familiar staples as eggs, butter, sugar, and flour. Common sense tells us that we should use the best available of these ingredients. Here you'll find a guide to choosing high-quality staples, and just after the basics you'll find other ingredients that have a natural affinity for salt in desserts, such as caramel, nuts, chocolate, and ale.

This book is not about using hard-to-find ingredients; however, a couple of recipes do use specialty ingredients that may not be easily located at your local grocery store. You'll find plenty of direction in the commentary in each recipe to lead you to the required ingredients. Most of them can be found at international markets or ordered online.

Butter: Unsalted butter (also called sweet butter) gives you complete control over the salt content in your baking, and it's important to use for recipes in this book. Salted butter should especially be avoided in recipes from the "Well-Seasoned" chapter (page 170) because those use all kinds of prepared salty treats as ingredients.

Chilled butter that is soft enough to yield to a finger pinch is indicative of a high moisture content, which means the butter is of inferior quality and can yield undesirable results in baked goods—so remember, the firmer the better.

Many of these recipes call for softened butter. It's best to allow butter to come to temper naturally, which means leaving it to stand at room temperature for 25 to 30 minutes or longer if needed. Properly softened butter will hold a finger indentation and still be slightly cold at its center, about 65°F/18°C. I once had a rule to never soften butter in the microwave, but I broke it so many times that I had to rethink my decorum. If you're in a hurry, you may choose to warm a stick of butter in the microwave for 5- to 10-second increments and at reduced power (50% or lower)—but you must first be very familiar with your microwave's heating idiosyncrasies. It's very easy to end up with a turntable of melted butter if you're not careful. Another option for speedy softening is to cut the butter into small pieces and let it stand until the desired softness is achieved.

Heavy whipping cream: Many of the recipes in this book use heavy whipping cream (also known as heavy cream). This cream contains 36 to 40 percent milk fat. The cream should be well chilled before you whip it. I prefer to whip the cream in a chilled stainless-steel bowl and with chilled mixer beaters. It whips easier and gains volume more quickly. When sweetening whipped cream, mix in the sugar when the cream is mostly whipped. It will achieve even higher volume.

Eggs: Pasteurized, grade A large eggs are recommended for recipes in this book. USDA eggs of this size and grade are about 2 ounces/55 g each. Farm-fresh eggs are a wonderful addition to recipes; they come in all sizes, so choose eggs close in size to large store-purchased eggs or weigh eggs before using. Because of the slight risk of salmonella, young children, the elderly, and others with a compromised immune system should avoid eating raw eggs.

In general, eggs should be brought to room temperature before adding them to batters, to achieve maximum volume and to prevent butter from resolidifying against the chilled eggs in the mixing bowl.

Flour: All-purpose flour is truly multipurpose, so I keep at least one bag in my pantry at all times. Use it in batter and dough, and as a thickener for puddings and pie fillings, and to dust work surfaces for rolling out pastries.

I use and recommend White Lily brand flour for pastries and cakes, and especially for the Bacon Fat Buttermilk Biscuits (page 142). I hesitate to say it's popular here in the South because it's more like a religion. It's the flour that generations of southerners (including my family) have used in their baking. The flour is made from low-gluten soft wheat, so it yields tender, fluffy baked goods. Many specialty food stores carry the flour,

but if you can't find it locally you can order it online. See Online Resources and Suppliers (page 228) for more information.

Whole wheat flour is another pantry staple I use for breads and pastries. It makes confections chewier, nutty-flavored, and a bit denser than those made with white flour. I occasionally use specialty flours, such as spelt and graham, for their unique flavors. These flours can be found easily at natural food stores and online.

Baking powder and baking soda: These should be checked for expiration dates before you begin your recipe. These leaveners lose their potency over time, and using an old product can result in dense and poorly risen confections.

Chocolate: Quality chocolate can be gauged by its ingredients; choose bar and block chocolates that contain cocoa butter. Some manufacturers replace cocoa butter with palm kernel oil or coconut oil; such chocolate costs less to make, but it is inferior quality and compromises flavor.

It's important to choose the right type of chocolate to use in a recipe. Bittersweet chocolate is assertive, so it should be used with strong, acidic flavors, such as citrus and berries. Semisweet chocolate is used most often in the recipes in this book. It has greater sugar content than bittersweet chocolate and is a good choice to keep stocked in your pantry. It works well in recipes as inclusions (chunks or pieces) and melted and mixed into batters. Milk chocolate is sweet and mild, and in some recipes, such as chocolate chip cookies, it can be substituted for semisweet chips. Take note if a recipe specifies "chocolate chips" or just "chocolate." Most chocolate chips have additives so they will hold their shape during baking, so they are not ideal for some recipes requiring a purer form of chocolate, or chocolate that needs to be melted.

I generally look for Fair Trade–certified chocolates because they are high quality and responsibly sourced, which means their cocoa farmers and producers are treated well and paid fairly. There is a misconception about Fair Trade products' being more expensive than their conventional counterparts. Fair Trade–certified chocolates and baking ingredients are priced competitively with gourmet and specialty ingredients of similar quality.

Caramel: Burnt sugar and sea salt complement each other remarkably. It's one of my favorite pairings, and you'll find that evident with the many caramel incarnations in this book. Among the recipes for scratch-made caramel sauces and candies, you'll find cookies and tarts that require ready-made caramel. Cajeta is one such caramel, made from goat's milk; it has a thick consistency and can be found in cans in the Latin American food section at grocery stores. Dulce de leche, which is made from cow's milk, can be substituted for cajeta in recipes.

Block caramel is softer than the cellophane-wrapped and bagged caramel pieces from the grocery store, and I recommend seeking out the former for inclusions in cookie batters and confections, or you can make your own block caramel with the soft block caramel recipe in this book (page 123). Otherwise, buy the best quality of these ingredients that you can find, or that your budget will allow.

Spirits and brews: The act of adding spirits to baked goods has been around since ancient times. Greeks and Romans added booze to cakes as a preservative, and the practice continued through medieval times. In addition to giving a long shelf life, it also imparts fine subtleties when used as an ingredient, and in such applications as soaking syrups and glazes, it delivers a tongue-tingling kick!

Many spirits used in this book tip to the sweet side and have a natural affinity with other sweet things. Rum, for example, is made from pure cane sugar, and is especially complementary to fruit and chocolate. Bourbon, made from sweet corn, hails from my beloved South and is an oft-used favorite in pound cake, pecan pie, and boozy whipped cream. In general, you should skip the really cheap stuff when purchasing booze for baking; choose spirits that you find pleasing to taste. The same goes for liqueurs, which are a mix of liquor and an extract or essence (think citrusy Cointreau or Grand Marnier). The bargain variety is sure to contain undesirable artificial flavorings; this is a concession made for unusually long shelf life. That said, there's no need to go broke buying top shelf. There are many fine affordable spirits to be discovered, so have fun testing a few.

For a while, baking with beer seemed to be limited to savory breads and stout cakes, but now I'm happy to find it in nearly every incarnation of dessert, including puddings, pies, candies, and tarts. Malt and hops are two flavor nuances that beer imparts when used as an ingredient, and it harmonizes well with the salt-sweet complement. You'll find plenty of beer and spirit-inspired recipes within these pages.

Coffee: I take full advantage of the affinity chocolate has with coffee. In chocolate cake and brownie recipes, a dose added to the batter adds flavor without having an overt coffee taste. You can replace the liquid (usually water or dairy) in many chocolaty recipes with a strong brew, to marvelous effect. That said, sometimes a less-gentle coffee flavor is desired, and that's when I turn to instant espresso powder. It's available at specialty food shops and Italian groceries (and online, of course). Usually the powder is dissolved in a small amount of hot water before being added to recipes. An acceptable substitute for espresso powder is freeze-dried coffee. It should also be dissolved in hot water before becoming an ingredient in batter and dough.

Nuts and nut butters: Nuts are a common ingredient in this book, as they are often a salty bite on their own. Use raw nuts for cookie dough add-ins and other recipes that are to be baked. At times, roasted salted nuts are called for, which can be purchased already prepared from the grocery store, though I recommend that you make them at home. It's easy and allows for more control over the salt and oil content in the finished confection. The method I use is called dry roasting, which uses no additional oil. Most nuts are already very rich with natural oils and those are expressed under heat. Smaller nuts and nut pieces will roast much quicker than whole nuts, so be sure to watch them carefully during baking. Considering the expense, burning them is a downright shame. If you are easily distracted, set a timer and check them after 5 minutes and thereafter at 1-minute intervals.

To roast nuts, preheat the oven to 350°F/180°C. Place the nuts in a single layer in a baking pan and bake for 5 minutes. Stir the nuts or shake the pan to promote even browning. Bake for 2 to 4 more minutes, until lightly browned and fragrant. Transfer the nuts to a bowl; toss with sea salt to taste (preferably fine-grain sel gris). If you're not sure about how much salt to use, a good ratio to follow is about 1 teaspoon of fine-grain sea salt to 1 pound/455 g of nuts.

There are many manufactured nut butters to choose from today, aside from the ubiquitous peanut butter. Cashew and almond butters can be substituted for peanut butter in most recipes, and vice versa. I love using natural nut butters. Perhaps you've used them, too, or have seen them in the produce section, usually with a thick layer of oil floating on the top. They may not look as appetizing on the shelf, but they contain no (or low) salt and sugar, and in my opinion that provides a more pure interpretation of the nut's flavor. These nut butters require stirring before use due to the separation of their natural oils. They also provide easier manipulation of the salt and sweet elements in a finished dessert. On the other side of the coin, there are no-stir traditional favorites that have been on the grocery store shelves for decades. They usually contain palm oil, which stabilizes the butter and reduces the separation of the natural oils—no stirring required. Although I prefer natural nut butter, I use whatever version will give me the end result I'm looking for. The types of nut butters I used in the recipes are specified as either "natural," which means free of additives, preservatives, or stabilizers, or "standard," which is no-stir, preseasoned, and sweetened, and most likely the variety you grew up with.

Vanilla beans: I use vanilla beans whenever possible in my confections, but boy, are they pricey! They cost much less in bulk, and you can easily purchase them online. I usually store the many beans in a large bottle of vodka; that way they stay nice and hydrated until I need to use them as an ingredient. I always return the used bean pods to the vodka bottle and in about three months' time I have a very large bottle of vanilla-infused vodka, which can be used in place of vanilla extract in recipes.

CHAPTER 1

A PINCH

Most baking recipes call for at least one pinch of salt, and if you've ever accidentally left out the ingredient, then you know even a slight amount is vitally important. It brightens flavors, enhances the subtleties, and truly makes dessert three-dimensional. Here, a modest amount of salt is used to leaven cakes and round out the flavor in confections. Rather than sprinkling it on top of desserts, it gets mixed in as an ingredient. It's like an undercover agent that seeks out the hidden secrets of otherwise bland-tasting ingredients and reports the findings to your taste buds. Finishing salts may be added to these sweets at your discretion.

Most of the recipes in this chapter use more than a literal "pinch" of salt, but the amount begs to be defined. How much is a pinch of salt? The short answer is the amount picked up or "pinched" between your thumb and forefinger, which is usually how I measure a pinch in my own kitchen when I cook. Baking, however, is more of an exact science, so the thumb-and-forefinger measurement is not the best method because it will vary from person to person. According to most sources today, a pinch is equal to ¹⁄₁₆ teaspoon, so it's a good idea to have a ¹⁄₁₆-teaspoon measure for accuracy. A good set of spoons will come with this measure, but it is not always included in all standard sets. If find you don't have this in your collection, you can fall back on the inexact thumb-and-forefinger pinch method, but next time you're shopping for home goods, consider picking up a new set of spoons that includes a ¹⁄₁₆-teaspoon measure (and probably a ¹⁄₈-teaspoon one as well). In my opinion, you can never have too many measuring spoons!

Fine-grain sea salt is a must for these recipes. I use and recommend a dry variety as opposed to those damp with briny sea water. As mentioned earlier in the "Salt Textures" chapter (page 19), fine-grain sea salt can be substituted in equal portions for table salt.

Caramel Buttermilk Tart with Cornmeal Crust

THIS RECIPE WAS INSPIRED BY MY family's tradition of eating cornbread in a glass of buttermilk. We crumble the cornbread right into a cold glass of buttermilk and eat it like cereal with a spoon. I'll admit, it's an acquired taste, but it's an old-time Appalachian practice that we never discarded despite how unfashionable it seems.

The base of this tart is a buttery cornmeal crust that provides an almost savory contrast to the silky, caramel-flavored buttermilk filling. (The filling, by the way, comes straight from Granny Baird's recipe card with my addition of goat's milk caramel to the batter. Hopefully she's looking down on my adjustment with approval.) The tart is finished with a generous dollop of black pepper whipped cream and a little more caramel drizzled on top. If you're looking to increase the salt-sweet contrast in this dessert, consider replacing the unsalted pecan pieces with roasted salted pecans.

There are two ready-made canned milk caramels that may be used for this recipe: cajeta and dulce de leche. I've found that there is some confusion when it comes to differentiating between the two. Cajeta is a milk caramel made with goat's milk, whereas dulce de leche is made with cow's milk. The former has a tangy flavor that enhances the buttermilk flavor in this tart, and I prefer it over dulce de leche in this recipe, but if you can't find cajeta, then dulce de leche is an excellent substitute.

{ INGREDIENTS }

Yields 8 to 10 servings

Cornmeal tart crust

1½ cups/180 g all-purpose flour

½ cup/90 g yellow cornmeal

¼ teaspoon fine-grain sea salt

1 tablespoon granulated sugar

4 ounces (1 stick)/110 g unsalted butter, cold, cubed

4 to 5 tablespoons water, ice cold

Caramel buttermilk filling

4 ounces (1 stick)/110 g unsalted butter, softened

1 cup/200 g granulated sugar

⅓ cup/80 ml cajeta or dulce de leche

2 tablespoons all-purpose flour

1/16 teaspoon fine-grain sea salt

3 large eggs

1 teaspoon pure vanilla extract

1 cup/240 ml buttermilk

Black pepper whipped cream

⅔ cup/160 ml heavy whipping cream

2 teaspoons granulated sugar

¼ teaspoon freshly ground black pepper

Cajeta drizzle

⅓ cup/80 ml cajeta

3 to 4 tablespoons heavy whipping cream

———

¼ cup/30 g chopped pecans (optional)

MAKE THE CORNMEAL TART CRUST

Combine the flour, cornmeal, salt, and sugar in the bowl of a food processor. Pulse the mixture in 1 or 2 short bursts to combine. Add the butter in a circle on top of the dry ingredients and pulse until the mixture resembles coarse meal with a few pea-size pieces of butter. Drizzle 4 tablespoons of cold water evenly over the mixture and pulse until just incorporated. Squeeze a handful of the mixture in the palm of your hand; the dough should hold together. If it doesn't hold or is very crumbly, add the remaining tablespoon of cold water and pulse again. When the dough passes the squeeze test, with floured hands, press it evenly into an ungreased tart pan. Cut away any excess dough from around the top of the pan and chill for 40 minutes.

Preheat the oven to 400°F/200°C.

Partially bake the tart crust for 7 minutes. Remove from the oven and let the tart crust cool completely in the pan.

Reduce the oven temperature to 325°F/165°C.

MAKE THE CARAMEL BUTTERMILK FILLING

Place the butter, sugar, and cajeta in a medium bowl and cream them together with an electric mixer on medium speed. Add the flour and salt. Add the eggs, one at a time, beating well after each addition. The mixture may look curdled, but don't be worried; this is normal. Reduce the mixer speed to low and add the vanilla and buttermilk. Mix until well incorporated.

Pour the pie filling into the parbaked cornmeal pie shell and bake for 50 minutes, or until a knife inserted into the center comes out clean.

Let the tart cool for 15 minutes before transferring it to the refrigerator to chill.

MAKE THE BLACK PEPPER WHIPPED CREAM

Place the heavy whipping cream in a medium bowl and beat it on high speed with an electric mixer until slightly thickened. With the mixer running, gradually add the sugar and then the black pepper. Continue to beat until the mixture is thick and fluffy. Pour the whipped cream into the center of the chilled pie.

MAKE THE CAJETA DRIZZLE

Place the cajeta and heavy whipping cream in a small saucepan. Heat over medium-low heat until the ingredients incorporate and can be stirred smooth. Let the mixture cool slightly, or until it stops steaming. Drizzle the cajeta mixture over the entire tart.

Sprinkle the pecan pieces (if using) around the top edge of the tart.

Serve immediately or store the tart, loosely covered in plastic wrap, in the refrigerator for up to 3 days.

Bananas Foster Belgian Waffle Sundaes

THIS DISH WALKS A FINE LINE BETWEEN breakfast and dessert. I'd like to believe it's both, but I'll leave that up to you to decide. Some would argue that the difference between the two is the scoop of ice cream on top. Others would quarrel that it's not proper to have rum before noon. While it's not a usual practice to eat either for breakfast, I can't say I'm against the notion. If you deem whipped cream a more fitting topping in the early hours, you'll hear no complaints from me. Or I'd suggest coffee ice cream in place of vanilla. As for the rum, most of the alcohol burns off during flambéing, so where breakfast is concerned, I say *flame on*!

Speaking of flames, let's keep them inside the pan. I've seen this dish cooked on a gas stovetop where the pan is tilted forward so the open flame is allowed to intermingle with the fumes. This causes the rum to ignite, which looks like sleight of hand, but it's a method best left to professionals. If you're not careful, the mixture may spill into the stove eye and cause a fire outside of the pan. Novices should use only a wand lighter.

Rum extract is a suitable substitution for dark rum in this recipe—there's no flambéing and just as delish.

Yields 4 to 8 servings

Belgian waffles

2 large eggs, separated

1 cup/120 g all-purpose flour

1 tablespoon baking powder

2 tablespoons granulated sugar

¼ teaspoon fine-grain sea salt

1 cup/240 g full-fat sour cream

¼ cup/60 ml half-and-half

¼ cup/60 ml grapeseed or peanut oil

1 teaspoon pure vanilla extract

Unsalted butter or nonstick cooking spray, for waffle iron

Bananas Foster topping

4 ounces (1 stick)/110 g unsalted butter

¼ cup/60 g firmly packed dark brown sugar

½ teaspoon ground cinnamon

½ cup/120 ml pure maple syrup

4 small firm, ripe bananas (about 15 ounces/ 430 g), sliced lengthwise and quartered

½ cup/50 g walnut pieces

¹⁄₁₆ teaspoon fine-grain sea salt

½ cup/120 ml dark rum, at room temperature, or 2 teaspoons rum extract

──────

Vanilla ice cream

∼ MAKE THE BELGIAN WAFFLES ∼

Preheat a Belgian waffle maker according to the manufacturer's instructions.

Beat the egg whites in a medium bowl with an electric mixer on high speed until stiff; set aside.

In a large bowl, whisk together the flour, baking powder, sugar, and salt. Add the sour cream and egg yolks to the flour mixture. Stir together with a wooden spoon until just combined. Add the half-and-half, oil, and vanilla; mix again with the wooden spoon until well combined. Fold in the egg whites with a large rubber spatula.

Grease the waffle iron with unsalted butter or lightly spray it with nonstick cooking spray. Pour ¾ cup/180 ml of batter into the waffle iron and let cook for 5 minutes or the manufacturer's suggested cooking time. Remove the waffle from the iron and repeat with the remaining batter. When all the batter is used, you should have four Belgian waffles, more or less, according to the size of your waffle maker. Set the waffles aside while you prepare the Bananas Foster topping.

MAKE THE BANANAS FOSTER TOPPING

Place the butter in a 10-inch/25.5 cm nonstick skillet over medium heat. When the butter has melted, add the brown sugar, cinnamon, and maple syrup. Stir to combine and cook until the sugar is dissolved and the mixture is syrupy, 5 to 7 minutes. Add the bananas and walnuts. Sprinkle the entire pan with the fine-grain salt and let the mixture bubble for 1 minute. Stir, then cook for 3 minutes longer, or until the bananas are glossy and coated in the syrup. If you choose not to use the rum, stir in the rum extract at this point.

If you are using the rum, pour it into the pan, and then very carefully lower an ignited wand lighter to the pan until the fumes cause the mixture to catch fire. Allow the mixture to flame until the alcohol burns off. This should take about 30 seconds. If the flame continues to burn for longer than 60 seconds, shake the pan to calm the flame until it is extinguished.

Place an entire waffle or half of one on a plate or in a fancy dessert glass. Pour the warm Bananas Foster mixture over the waffle and top with a big scoop of vanilla ice cream (or coffee ice cream—so good!). Repeat with the remaining waffles. Serve immediately.

The waffles can be made ahead and frozen. Store the waffles between sheets of parchment paper in large, resealable freezer bags with the air removed. Reheat them in the oven at 350°F/180°C for 10 minutes, or allow them to thaw at room temperature and crisp them in 1 tablespoon of unsalted melted butter (each) in a nonstick skillet.

Scratch-made waffles like these will take a little extra effort, but I promise you they are well worth it. You can shortcut this recipe by making waffles from a baking mix or with those newfangled "shake and pour" batter jugs, but I can't wholeheartedly recommend it.

Chilled rum will lower the temperature of the ingredients in the pan and slow the cooking process. It may also hinder ignition, so be sure the alcohol is room temperature before using.

Black Sesame Cupcakes with Matcha Buttercream

I NEVER IMAGINED CALLING A CUPCAKE sophisticated, but I think this one deserves that description. It's made with refined ingredients—black sesame paste and matcha tea powder.

The Japanese have long used black sesame seeds in their desserts, which tend to be less sweet than their American counterparts. I've found that the seeds have wonderfully smoky undertones that contrast nicely with the more obvious sweetness in Western desserts.

Sweet black sesame paste is used in the cake portion of this recipe. You can purchase black sesame paste ready-made at international grocery stores, but the best version is homemade, and you can make your own with the recipe provided. I add a pinch of fine-grain salt to the paste and it nicely punctuates the smoky flavor.

Recently matcha green tea powder has gained popularity as an ingredient in desserts,

and I am its biggest fan. The finely powdered bright green tea gives vibrancy to all kinds of confections. Like black sesame seeds, matcha has an earthy flavor, so the two complement each other well.

Matcha tea is produced in several different grades. Culinary grade should be used for baking because it provides the flavor we seek without the expensive price tag of the ceremonial-grade matcha. Culinary matcha can be found at specialty tea shops and ordered online.

Admittedly, this recipe has several steps, especially if you make your own black sesame paste to use in the cake recipe. I usually whip these up in one day—black sesame paste and all—but if you're feeling overwhelmed, spread the work out over the course of two days. Prepare the black sesame paste the first day, and make the cupcakes and icing on the second day.

{ INGREDIENTS }

Yields 15 cupcakes

Black sesame cupcakes

4 ounces (1 stick)/110 g unsalted butter, softened

1 cup/200 g granulated sugar

2 large eggs

2 teaspoons pure vanilla extract

1¾ cups/210 g all-purpose flour

½ teaspoon baking soda

½ teaspoon baking powder

¼ teaspoon fine-grain sea salt

1 cup/90 g black sesame paste (recipe follows)

Matcha Swiss buttercream frosting

6 large egg whites

1 cup/200 g granulated sugar

1/16 teaspoon fine-grain sea salt

1 pound plus 4 tablespoons (5 sticks)/570 g unsalted butter, cubed and softened

2 teaspoons pure vanilla extract

½ teaspoon almond extract

1 tablespoon matcha green tea powder, sifted, plus more for garnish

1½ tablespoons hot water (about 170°F/77°C)

---

15 to 30 matcha-flavored Pocky sticks, for garnish (optional)

MAKE THE BLACK SESAME CUPCAKES

Preheat the oven to 350°F/180°C. Line 15 wells of a standard cupcake pan with paper liners.

In the bowl of an electric mixer fitted with the paddle attachment, cream together the butter and sugar until light and fluffy. Add the eggs, one at a time, beating well after each addition. Add the vanilla and mix again. Whisk together the flour, baking soda, baking powder, and salt, set aside. Add the flour mixture and black sesame paste alternately to the butter mixture, beginning and ending with the flour mixture. The batter will be thick.

Fill the cupcake liners with ¼-cup/60 g level measures of the batter. Bake for 17 to 22 minutes. Allow the cupcakes to cool completely on a cooling rack.

MAKE THE MATCHA SWISS BUTTERCREAM FROSTING

Set a saucepan filled one-third full of water over medium-high heat and bring to a simmer.

Whisk together the egg whites, sugar, and salt in a large, heatproof bowl. Set the bowl over the simmering water and whisk until the mixture is hot to the touch and the sugar has dissolved.

Transfer the mixture to the bowl of an electric mixer fitted with the whisk attachment.

Beat on low speed for 2 minutes. Increase the speed to medium-high and beat until stiff peaks are formed.

Continue to beat at medium-high speed until the mixture is fluffy and has cooled (the mixing bowl should feel cool to the touch).

Turn off the mixer and switch from the whisk attachment to the paddle. Turn the mixer on medium-low speed and add the butter, a few cubes at a time, beating until well incorporated before the next addition. The egg whites will deflate and thin with the first few additions. Don't let this discourage you; just keep at it. The mixture may also look curdled, but don't fret over that, either. Beat the mixture at high speed when all the butter has been added. The mixture will thicken and become smooth after several minutes of beating. Beat in the vanilla and almond extracts. Place the matcha tea powder and hot water in a small bowl and stir until a smooth paste forms. If the mixture is very thick, add more hot water until it is very smooth but not too liquidy. Add the matcha paste to the batter and beat until the frosting is completely smooth and consistently green in color.

Smooth the frosting onto the cooled cupcakes with an offset spatula, or transfer the frosting to a piping bag fitted with a decorator's large star piping tip; pipe the frosting onto the cupcakes in a large swirl. Place 1 or 2 matcha-flavored Pocky sticks (if using) on each cupcake. Sift a pinch of matcha tea powder over each cupcake, if desired.

Matcha green tea powder must be sifted before use. It has an extremely fine consistency similar to that of unsweetened cocoa powder, and static electricity will sometimes make the powder stick together in little clumps. If you've ever made a cup of hot cocoa without sifting the cocoa powder first, then you've probably experienced clumps of powder that rise to the top after the hot milk is added to the cup. No matter how much you stir, those little clumps are determined to cling together. The same thing happens with matcha tea powder, so sifting is very important. Failing to sift the matcha in this recipe will yield an uneven speckled frosting with clumps of matcha powder throughout.

The chocolate-covered biscuit sticks known as Pocky are a popular Japanese snack. You can find them at international grocery stores and specialty markets. They come in all kinds of flavors, such as strawberry, blueberry, milk chocolate, and the matcha green tea version I've used in this recipe.

BLACK SESAME PASTE

Sweet black sesame paste is often served alone as a dessert, but I use it to create black sesame confections. You'll need a blender to make this recipe, with high settings of liquefy or purée to grind the seeds finely. I've found that my food processor does not work as well at grinding the sesame seeds. You'll also need glutinous rice flour, which is stickier than regular rice flour and sold at international markets. To be sure you're getting the right product, look for the word *mochiko* on the rice flour packaging. There are no substitutes for this special rice flour, so I'll say it again for emphasis—be sure it says mochiko on the box.

─┤ INGREDIENTS ├─

Yields about 1²/₃ cups/450 g paste

½ cup/80 g black sesame seeds

¼ cup/50 g granulated sugar

¹/₁₆ teaspoon fine-grain sea salt

¼ cup/30 g glutinous rice flour (*mochiko*)

2 cups/480 ml cold water

In a saucepan over medium heat, toast the sesame seeds. Stir constantly to prevent burning. It's difficult to see whether black sesame seeds are toasted, so heat them only until they become fragrant.

Place the toasted seeds, sugar, salt, and glutinous rice flour in a blender. Add 1 cup/240 ml of the cold water. Blend together on the PURÉE or LIQUEFY setting until you cannot see any whole sesame seeds. This may take up to 10 minutes.

Transfer the blended mixture to a saucepan and add the remaining cup/240 ml of cold water. Bring to a boil over medium-high heat, whisking constantly. The mixture will thicken quickly and become very dark. Remove the pan from the heat source when the mixture is thick and has a pasty consistency. Let the sesame paste cool completely before using it in confections.

Toasted Coconut Bourbon Marshmallows

I'VE OFTEN REFERRED TO THESE marshmallows as "Wild Turkey in the Straw," a kind of homage to the old jug band tune and a favorite brand of bourbon to bake with, Wild Turkey. The "straw" is a nod to the toasted coconut coating. I really love how the contrasting textures of fluffy marshmallow and crisp golden coconut harmonize in this dessert.

Kentucky bourbon is made with corn mash, which gives it a sweetness that goes well in these marshmallows and all kinds of other desserts (e.g., the Bourbon Brown Sugar Pound Cake, page 70). If you're not inclined to use Kentucky bourbon in these mallows, then you may use whiskey, if you prefer, or if that's what you have on hand. However, I'd like to make a case for spirits that hail from the South because they are both tasty and affordable. Jack Daniel's

Tennessee whiskey is a suitable substitute to use in this dessert. Like Kentucky bourbon, it is made with sweet corn. Both spirits are strong and permeate sweets to give them nuances of vanilla, oak, and caramel flavor.

My baking peer Shauna Sever of the popular *Piece of Cake* blog taught me how to make the best homemade marshmallows with her book *Marshmallow Madness!* I consult it whenever I'm dreaming up new flavor combinations, and I altered her base recipe to create these bourbon marshmallows. Unlike most homemade marshmallow recipes, this one does not use egg whites (which tend to weep and make a soggy mess of mallows if not whipped and tempered properly). Instead, this recipe uses unflavored gelatin and boiled sugar syrup, so it is more forgiving and easier for novice marshmallow makers to find success.

{ INGREDIENTS }

Yields 24 marshmallows

Neutral-tasting nonstick cooking spray, for pan

Gelatin base

½ cup/120 ml cold water

2 tablespoons Kentucky bourbon (I like Wild Turkey)

5 teaspoons powdered unflavored gelatin

Sugar syrup

¾ cup/150 g granulated sugar

½ cup/160 g light corn syrup, divided

2 tablespoons Kentucky bourbon

¼ teaspoon fine-grain sea salt

Coating

½ cup/60 g confectioners' sugar

3 tablespoons cornstarch

1 cup/240 g sweetened shredded coconut, toasted

6 ounces/170 g semisweet chocolate, finely chopped

Flake sea salt, optional

Prepare an 8 x 8-inch/20 x 20 cm baking pan by lightly spraying it with a neutral-tasting non-stick cooking spray.

⌐ MAKE THE GELATIN BASE ⌐

Combine the cold water and bourbon in a small bowl; whisk in the gelatin and let stand until set.

⌒ MAKE THE SUGAR SYRUP ⌒

Stir together the sugar, ¼ cup/80 g of the corn syrup, ¼ cup/60 ml of water, bourbon, and salt in a medium saucepan. Clip a candy thermometer to the side of the pan. Place the saucepan over high heat and bring to a boil; cook until the mixture reaches 240°F/115°C.

While you wait for the sugar syrup to come to a boil, heat the gelatin mixture in a microwave at 100% power for 30 seconds, or until the gelatin is liquefied. Pour the gelatin mixture into an electric mixer bowl fitted with the whisk attachment. Add the remaining ¼ cup of corn syrup to the bowl. Turn the mixer on low speed and keep it running.

When the sugar syrup reaches 240°F/115°C, remove it from the heat source and slowly pour it into the gelatin mixture in a thin stream. Increase the mixer speed to medium and, with a timer set, beat for 5 minutes. After 5 minutes, increase the mixer speed to high and beat for 5 to 7 more minutes, or until thick and opaque.

Spray a rubber spatula with the nonstick cooking spray.

When the mixture has tripled in volume, pour it into the prepared pan and smooth the top with the rubber spatula. Let stand until set, about 4 hours, or until the marshmallow is firm and spongy.

⌒ MAKE THE COATING ⌒

Combine the confectioners' sugar and cornstarch in a small bowl. Generously dredge a work surface with some of the mixture. Use a knife to loosen the marshmallow from the edges of the pan. Turn out the marshmallow onto the work surface. Cut the marshmallow slab into pieces roughly 1½ inches/4 cm square.

Dredge each piece in the remaining confectioners' sugar mixture.

Cover a work surface with nonstick kitchen paper, such as waxed paper or parchment paper.

Place the toasted coconut in a small bowl; set aside. Melt the chopped chocolate in a small bowl in the microwave at 100% power at 30-second intervals until it can be stirred smooth. Dip an end of each marshmallow in chocolate and then in the coconut; place it on the paper. Repeat with the remaining marshmallows. Sprinkle the chocolate-dipped end of each marshmallow with flake sea salt, if using. Allow the chocolate-dipped marshmallows to stand at room temperature for about 2 hours, or until the chocolate is set.

Wrap the marshmallows in cellophane bags tied with raffia for a pretty gift, or display them in cupcake liners on a large serving tray when entertaining.

Store the marshmallows in an airtight container.

Toasting coconut is easy. Spread it in an even layer over an ungreased baking sheet (about 15 x 10 inches/38 x 25 cm) and bake for 8 minutes at 350°F/180°C, checking and stirring it often for even browning.

Ricotta-Fig Phyllo Cups

MY GRANDMOTHER LOVED ALL THINGS miniature. She bought tiny bantam roosters to roam her farmyard (for her own amusement, I firmly believe), patted out tiny biscuits for herself at breakfast, and collected a mishmash of tiny cups and plates. She'd often eat dinner on a plate the size of a teacup saucer. I found that both confounding and endearing.

I share her love of petite serving ware (I have a mishmash of my own)—and little desserts are my greatest love in miniature. These filled phyllo cups are a prime example.

The phyllo cups for this dessert can be made a few days ahead and stored in an airtight container until you're ready to use them. If you're serving these to dinner guests, have all the components ready ahead of time. In addition to having the phyllo cups ready, prepare the cream cheese filling, chop the nuts, and quarter the figs, then put everything together just before serving. It only takes a couple of minutes to assemble these desserts, and you can be confident that the phyllo cup will stay crisp and lovely.

{ INGREDIENTS }

Yields 6 servings

Unsalted butter, for ramekins

1/2 cup/120 g whole-milk ricotta cheese

1/4 cup/60 ml heavy whipping cream

2 tablespoons granulated sugar

1/2 teaspoon pure vanilla extract

1/16 teaspoon fine-grain sea salt

6 sheets of frozen phyllo dough, thawed (18 x 14 inches/45.5 x 35.5 cm each)

3 tablespoons/50 g unsalted butter, melted

12 fresh figs, quartered

6 tablespoons chopped walnuts, toasted

1/2 cup/170 g wildflower honey

Preheat the oven to 350°F/180°C.

Butter six 8-ounce/240 ml round ramekins and set aside.

Place the ricotta and heavy whipping cream in a medium mixing bowl. Beat the mixture on medium speed with an electric mixer, gradually adding the sugar, until the mixture is thickened to soft peaks. Add the vanilla and salt; mix well. Cover the mixture and chill while the other elements are prepared.

Stack 2 phyllo sheets on a work surface and cover the remaining sheets with a damp paper towel to prevent the dough from drying. Brush the sheets evenly with some of the melted butter. Top the buttered phyllo sheets with 2 more sheets of phyllo and brush with butter as before. Top with the last 2 phyllo sheets and gently press all the layers together.

Cut the phyllo stacks into six 7 x 6-inch/18 x 15 cm rectangles. Carefully fit a rectangle of phyllo into each buttered ramekin, creating a phyllo cup. The phyllo will slightly extend over the top of each ramekin. Place the ramekins on a baking sheet and transfer to the oven. Bake for 20 minutes, or until the phyllo dough cups are crisp and golden. Allow the phyllo cups to cool for 5 minutes inside the ramekins, then gently remove them and place them on a cooling rack. The cups may also be kept inside the ramekins for serving, if you prefer.

Just before serving, divide the ricotta mixture evenly among the cups. Top each basket with 2 quartered figs. Sprinkle 1 tablespoon of toasted walnut pieces over each cup and drizzle each cup with honey. Serve immediately.

Brandy Snaps with Orange Liqueur Cream

I'M USUALLY MET WITH A PUZZLED look when I tell people these are homemade. They don't believe me. I try to tell explain that there's no wizardry in creating perfect tubular casings with flour and sugar. The only special tool needed is a wooden spoon or whisk, and not the business end, at that.

The cookies start out as syrupy batter and after they're baked they're flat and shiny, almost like plastic. After shaping them around a spoon handle, the result is crisp cigars that snap and shatter when bitten. Underbaked snaps won't snap at all. Instead they'll be chewy and collapse between the teeth. If you're new to making these, I recommend testing the first batch by breaking a cookie in half after it has had plenty of time to firm. If it snaps and shatters, then the cookies are appropriately baked. If chewy and bendy, then increase the bake time by 2 to 3 minutes and try again.

These seem to cross the line from cookie to pastry after they're filled with the orange liqueur whipped cream. The "brandy" in brandy snaps refers to the color of the cookies. For those disappointed to find no brandy in the cookie, feel free to substitute your favorite flavored brandy for the orange liqueur in the whipped filling.

The first time I made brandy snaps, I congratulated myself a bit too soon on a job well done. The preparation went well, but presentation—not so much. I filled them just before an hour drive to our Christmas Eve shindig, and then they sat on the buffet for 2 more hours. The snaps were falling apart from the moisture in the whipped cream by the time guests were trying to put them on their plates, much to my chagrin. But everyone was digging in anyway, with spoons, which is a testament to how delicious these cookies are. To avoid my party faux pas, fill the brandy snaps just before serving. You can also fill them up to 2 hours before serving and store them in the refrigerator. Or do as I often do: Serve the whipped cream and cookies on a chip-and-dip service set and allow the guests to dip the cookies into the cream (but no double dipping allowed!).

{ INGREDIENTS }

Yields 24 cookies

Cookies

3½ tablespoons/50 g unsalted butter

⅓ cup/70 g firmly packed dark brown sugar

¼ cup/80 g molasses

⅓ cup/40 g all-purpose flour, sifted

1/16 teaspoon fine-grain sea salt

Whipped cream

1½ cups/360 ml heavy whipping cream

3 tablespoons granulated sugar

2 tablespoons orange liqueur (I like Grand Marnier)

MAKE THE COOKIES

Preheat the oven to 350°F/180°C.

Line a large baking sheet (16 x 14 inches/40 x 36 cm or larger) with parchment paper or a silicone baking mat.

In a medium saucepan, combine the butter, brown sugar, and molasses. Place the pan over medium heat. Cook the mixture for about 5 minutes, or until the butter and sugar are melted and can be stirred together. Remove the pan from the heat source.

Stir the flour and salt into the melted mixture. Scoop the mixture by the level teaspoonful and place it on the prepared baking sheet. Drop no more than 4 teaspoons of batter, well spaced, onto the baking sheet. Bake the cookie batter for 7 to 9 minutes, or until the cookies are bubbling and have spread to about 4 inches/10 cm in diameter. If the batter starts to firm and becomes difficult to drop from a teaspoon, place the pan over low heat until the mixture relaxes, then remove it from the heat source and continue to spoon it out as before.

Remove the cookies from the oven and allow them to cool on the baking sheet for 2 to 3 minutes, or until each cookie can be peeled away from the liner in 1 piece (much like window cling film), and is still flexible. Working quickly, wrap each cookie around the handle of a wooden spoon or whisk (the handle should be about 1 inch/2.5 cm in diameter). Hold the cookie on the spoon handle for about 1 minute, then gently slide it off and place the cookie on a cooling rack. Repeat with the remaining cookies.

Continue to bake more spoonsful of the batter as before, until all the batter is used.

MAKE THE WHIPPED CREAM

Beat the heavy whipping cream in a large bowl with an electric mixer on medium-high speed. When the cream begins to thicken, gradually add the sugar, 1 tablespoon at a time. Finally, add the orange liqueur and beat until stiff peaks form. Serve the whipped cream beside the tray full of brandy snaps, or transfer the cream to a piping bag and fill the cookies just before serving.

If you are an avid baker and have cannoli forms in your bakeware arsenal, then use them for shaping these cookies.

Bourbon Brown Sugar Pound Cake

I LIKE TO SERVE THIS CAKE IN THE FALL when the weather turns brisk, but I've also been known to gift it at Christmastime to friends and neighbors. You can make it a couple of days ahead of time because it improves upon standing. The bourbon becomes fully developed and mellow, and the cake's crumb settles into a dense, velvety texture. It's perfectly casual and homey feeling for weeknight baking, but if you use a fancy Bundt pan it's not too dowdy for company. The cinnamon-sugar mixture adds even more eye appeal, and because the cake is sticky with a buttery whiskey sauce, the sugar clings to the surface in an even layer.

There's just one important thing I have to address: Fancy Bundt pans can be a real pain to grease and flour. I've seen Bundt pans shaped like Christmas wreaths and cathedrals—all with a stunning amount of detail. All that detail means there are plenty of nooks and crannies to grease and flour, and missing a single crevice can cause the cake to stick inside the pan. To avoid such an atrocity, I suggest using a flour-based baking spray to grease and flour the pan in one easy step (see Online Resources and Suppliers, page 218). You can find this spray in the baking aisle at the grocery store with the other nonstick cooking sprays. It does a good job of getting efficiently into all those fluted edges and ridges, and it ensures the cake releases easily from the pan in one flawless piece.

An important step is to rest the cake for 5 minutes before turning it out of the pan. This allows the cake to pull away from the bottom and sides of the pan as heat is released. Dark-coated Bundt pans will retain heat and continue to cook the cake outside the oven, so it's especially important to turn out the cake right at the 5-minute mark. Allowing the cake to sit in the pan for an extended period of time can cause the outside to overcook and develop a hard crust, and nobody wants that.

{ INGREDIENTS }

Yields 12 servings

Pound cake

Unsalted butter and flour, or flour-based baking spray, for pan

8 ounces (2 sticks)/230 g unsalted butter, softened

1½ cups/330 g firmly packed dark brown sugar

½ cup/100 g granulated sugar

5 large eggs

2 teaspoons pure vanilla extract

¼ cup/60 ml Kentucky bourbon (I like Wild Turkey)

3 cups/360 g all-purpose flour

¾ teaspoon fine-grain sea salt

½ teaspoon baking powder

½ teaspoon baking soda

¾ cup/180 ml buttermilk

Butter-whiskey syrup

⅓ cup/70 g granulated sugar

4 tablespoons (½ stick)/60 g unsalted butter

1/16 teaspoon fine-grain sea salt

¼ cup/60 ml Kentucky bourbon

Cinnamon-sugar coating

¼ cup/50 g granulated sugar

1 teaspoon ground cinnamon

1/16 teaspoon fine-grain salt

⌒ MAKE THE POUND CAKE ⌒

Preheat the oven to 325°F/165°C.

Butter and flour a 12-cup/4.2 L Bundt pan, or spray the pan with a flour-based baking spray.

Place the butter, brown sugar, and granulated sugar in a large mixing bowl. Beat at medium speed with an electric mixer until creamy and no lumps of sugar remain, about 5 minutes. Add the eggs, one at a time, beating well with each addition. Beat in the vanilla and whiskey. When the mixture is thoroughly combined, turn off the mixer and set the bowl aside.

In a separate bowl, whisk together the flour, salt, baking powder, and baking soda. Turn the mixer on low speed and beat in the flour mixture and buttermilk alternately, beginning and ending with the flour mixture.

Pour the batter into the prepared pan. Bake for 1 hour, or until a toothpick inserted into the center of the cake comes out clean. Allow the cake to cool in the pan for 5 minutes. Turn out the cake onto a cooling rack to cool completely. Place the cooling rack atop a large baking sheet.

MAKE THE BUTTER-WHISKEY SYRUP

Combine the sugar, butter, and ¼ cup/60 ml of water in a small saucepan and place over medium heat. Stir until the sugar melts, about 5 minutes. Remove the pan from the heat source and stir in the whiskey and salt.

Brush the syrup over the surface of the cooled cake liberally using a pastry brush, or pour the syrup over the cake a little at a time, until all the syrup is used.

MAKE THE CINNAMON-SUGAR COATING

In a small bowl, stir together the sugar, cinnamon, and salt, and sprinkle over the entire cake, allowing the excess to fall onto the baking sheet. Transfer the cake from the cooling rack to a cake stand or serving platter, using a cake lifter or 2 spatulas. Serve the cake immediately or wrap it in plastic wrap and store it at room temperature for up to 48 hours before serving.

Store the cake at room temperature, covered in plastic wrap.

Although I strongly suggest seeking out the real thing, there's a buttermilk substitute that's accessible and easy to make. Combine 1 cup/240 ml of milk or heavy whipping cream with 1 tablespoon of freshly squeezed lemon juice or white vinegar. Let the mixture stand at room temperature for 5 to 10 minutes. You'll know it's ready when it thickens and slightly curdles. Use this substitute in equal measure to the buttermilk called for in a recipe. This substitute is best used in bread or cake batters. It is not as thick or tangy as real buttermilk, so it is not a suitable substitute for the buttermilk in the Caramel Buttermilk Tart (page 42).

Hibiscus Tea Gelée and Cream

THE BERRY-RICH FLAVOR OF HIBISCUS tea never ceases to amaze me. It tastes like a combination of raspberry and tart cranberry with something floral lingering in the background. It's good in all kinds of sweets so I use it whenever I can in my confectionery.

Here, hibiscus tea is mixed with grenadine syrup and made into a sweet jelly. The bright pomegranate flavor of grenadine complements hibiscus perfectly. Good grenadine is made with real pomegranate juice. You may have trouble finding real grenadine at the grocery store (and no trouble at all finding the artificial kind), but it is available at most kitchen specialty shops and online.

As the hibiscus is Hawaii's state flower, it only seemed right to use a pinch of Hawaiian red alaea salt as a topping. It's delicious on cream and makes an eye-catching finish.

{ INGREDIENTS }

Yields six 5-ounce/150 ml servings

1 tablespoon powdered unflavored gelatin

3 tablespoons cold water

1½ cups/360 ml steeped hibiscus tea, hot

½ cup/120 ml grenadine syrup, at room temperature

1 cup/240 ml heavy whipping cream

3 tablespoons granulated sugar

Hawaiian red alaea salt

In a small condiment cup, stir together the powdered gelatin and cold water. Let stand until set, about 2 minutes.

Place the bloomed gelatin in the hot hibiscus tea; stir until the gelatin is completely melted. Add the grenadine syrup and stir to combine. Evenly divide the mixture among six 5-ounce/150 ml dessert cups and cover the jelly cups with plastic wrap. Place each cup, tilted, in a cavity of an egg carton and transfer the carton to the refrigerator. Let the hibiscus jelly chill until set, about 45 minutes.

Place the heavy whipping cream in a large bowl and beat with an electric mixer on high speed. When the mixture starts to thicken, gradually add the sugar 1 tablespoon at a time. Beat the mixture until thick but still pourable.

Divide the cream among the dessert cups, tapping each cup on a work surface to remove any air bubbles. Cover and refrigerate the cups until ready to serve.

Just before serving, garnish each cup with a pinch of alaea salt.

Butterscotch Budino Tiramisu

USUALLY THE FIRST THING THAT COMES to mind at the word *butterscotch* is a bag of chalky tan baking chips. Forget about that artifice for now (or forevermore, if possible). The genesis of butterscotch was a hard candy made from unprocessed sugar, but it has evolved into something much more caramel-like and pourable. Today, authentic butterscotch is simply made with cream, brown sugar, and butter.

Now add to this list a shot of single malt Scotch. Not because it's canon (it's not) but because it makes all incarnations of butterscotch transcendent. I find it a crucial element for this very butterscotch pudding (or *budino*—that means "pudding" in Italian, and since we're making tiramisu . . . well, you get it). Just a little

bit makes a huge difference in flavor, and even though you might look at the recipe and consider omitting the meager 2 tablespoons called for, I'd ask you to reconsider. There's really no substitute for it, unless you have leftover Kentucky bourbon from making marshmallows (page 59) or Bourbon Brown Sugar Pound Cake (page 70). It's the only replacement I can recommend in good conscience.

Like most tiramisu recipes, this one is layered with *savoiardi* (ladyfingers) and topped with luscious homemade whipped cream. The coffee flavor is punched up with a sprinkle of espresso powder on top. If you don't have any on hand, freeze-dried instant coffee can be ground fine in a food processor and used in its place.

{ INGREDIENTS }

Yields 4 servings

16 pieces/90 g crisp ladyfinger biscuits

¾ cup/180 ml freshly brewed coffee

½ cup/110 g firmly packed dark brown sugar

2 tablespoons cornstarch

1/16 teaspoon fine-grain sea salt

2 cups/480 ml whole milk

2 large egg yolks, lightly beaten

4 tablespoons (½ stick)/60 g unsalted butter

2 tablespoons single malt Scotch whiskey (I like Jameson)

1 cup/240 ml heavy whipping cream

2 tablespoons granulated sugar

¼ cup/30 g unsweetened cocoa powder

½ teaspoon espresso powder

Chop the ladyfinger biscuits into 1-inch/2.5 cm pieces and layer them equally in the bottoms of four 7- to 8-ounce/207 to 237 ml glass jars or dessert cups (7.2-ounce/213 ml Weck glass jars are pictured). Divide the coffee evenly among the jars, sprinkling it over the biscuits with a spoon. Set the jars aside while you prepare the pudding.

Whisk the brown sugar, cornstarch, and salt together in a 2½-quart/2.4 L saucepan. Add the milk and egg yolks and stir until smooth. Cook, stirring with a whisk, over medium-high heat until the mixture comes to a boil. This will take 5 to 7 minutes, depending on the gauge of metal your saucepan (heavier-bottomed saucepans will take longer to heat). Continue to cook, whisking moderately and constantly, until the mixture has thickened considerably, 3 to 5 minutes more. Remove the pan from the heat source and add the butter 1 tablespoon at a time until melted. Whisk in the whiskey. Continue to whisk for 3 to 5 minutes, or until the pudding cools enough to stop steaming. You may transfer the pudding to a bowl to speed this process. Divide the pudding evenly among the jars, about ½ cup/110 g per jar and cover the puddings with plastic wrap. Transfer the jars to the refrigerator and allow the pudding to set, about 1 hour.

For the whipped topping, beat the heavy whipping cream with the granulated sugar until stiff peaks form. Whisk together the cocoa powder and espresso powder. Top each pudding with the whipped cream and sprinkle with the cocoa mixture. Serve the cups chilled. Store leftovers, covered in plastic wrap, in the refrigerator.

To make the fork stencil: *Top the jars with whipped cream until overflowing and then scrape the excess with an offset spatula so that the cream is level with the rim of the jar. Hold the head of a small fork over each jar as you sieve the cocoa mixture over the whipped cream. Serve immediately.*

CHAPTER 2

JUST A SPRINKLE

This chapter turns up the dial a little by making salt more prominent. Here you'll find flake salt sitting on top of ganache or coarse grains adorning slushy granita. Sprinkling salt on top of a sweet is one of the best ways you can appreciate the flavor and texture of sea salt.

All the recipes in this chapter will allow you to stretch your creativity with your choice of salts. Since it is utilized as a dramatic finish, you can mix and match your favorites. It's easy to swap out Hawaiian black lava salt for fleur de sel or any other sea salt you have stashed in your cupboard. I love experimenting with textures by combining flake salt with crystals before adding it as a garnish, and you should try it, too. And if you're feeling highly creative, it's fun to use your own exciting flavors of finishing salts from the "DIY Sea Salts" chapter (page 214).

"Just a sprinkle" could be a pinch on top of a cupcake or two to three pinches over an entire batch of butter toffee. Remember, a pinch is equal to $1/16$ teaspoon, so if you're not sure how much salt to sprinkle on top of a confection, start with a pinch and increase the amount to taste.

My last and most important words for finishing a dessert with salt: It's better to add salt a little at a time to a confection because, most often, you can't unsalt what you've salted. It's a good idea to taste the salt you're going to use to gauge its texture and flavor. I've said it before, but it bears repeating: coarse salt has staying power, and provides a hefty burst of salinity, so it should be used sparingly. Also keep in mind that extra-fine salts (velvet salts) are the consistency of flour, so a little bit goes a long way. They should also be used in small amounts.

Espresso Mousse Soufflés with Fleur de Sel

SOME PEOPLE SWEAR BY A PINCH OF salt in their coffee—some take it in the cup and others put it in the grounds before brewing. The claim is that it tempers the bitterness of a sub-par brew, and as an occasional coffee salter I tend to agree. This dessert was inspired by that act more so than by the outcome, but a sprinkle of fine-grain salt during preparation helps bring this dessert to full flavor potential. These cold mousse cups are rich and fluffy; a small but potent dessert prepared in 3-ounce/9 ml demitasses (demitasses are small cups in which espresso is served). Instead of the usual sprinkle of fleur de sel, these occasionally receive a garnish of Hawaiian black lava salt, so use whatever coarse salt you prefer.

Now, I'll understand if you bypass the stand-up collar method that helps give this mousse its stately height. It's not a complicated task, but it does require an extra step and parchment paper. If you choose to serve the mousse in fancy martini glasses instead, the result will be no less delicious. Having said that, I don't consider the chocolate garnish on top optional.

{ INGREDIENTS }

Yields 6 servings

2 tablespoons/30 ml cold water

1 (¼-ounce/7 g) package) powdered unflavored gelatin

2 large egg yolks

½ cup/100 g granulated sugar

2 tablespoons instant espresso powder

1/16 teaspoon ground cinnamon

1/16 teaspoon fine-grain sea salt

1⅓ cups/390 ml whole milk

1 teaspoon pure vanilla extract

1½ cups/360 ml heavy whipping cream

Chocolate curls or shavings

Fleur de sel or Hawaiian red alaea salt

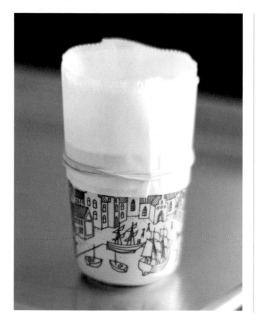

Make a stand-up collar for 6 demitasse cups by wrapping a strip of parchment paper around each cup so that the strip stands about 2 inches/5 cm above the rim of the cup. Secure the paper with a thick rubber band.

Place the cold water in a small, micro-wave-safe bowl. Sprinkle the powdered gelatin evenly over the surface of the water. Let stand until the gelatin is absorbed. Set aside.

Set a saucepan filled one-third full with water over medium-high heat and bring to a simmer. Whisk together the egg yolks, sugar, espresso powder, cinnamon, salt, and milk in a large, heatproof bowl. Place the bowl over the pan of simmering water and whisk constantly for 3 minutes. Microwave the gelatin at 100%

power for 5 to 10 seconds, or until it turns to liquid. Add the liquid gelatin to the egg yolk mixture and whisk for 7 minutes more, or until slightly thickened. Remove the bowl from the simmering water and stir in the vanilla. Place the bowl in a larger bowl filled with ice water to speed setting. Stir occasionally until the mixture is as thick as unbeaten egg whites.

In a separate bowl, beat the heavy whipping cream to stiff peaks with an electric mixer. Fold the whipped cream into the coffee mixture with a rubber spatula until no white streaks remain. Spoon the mousse mixture evenly into the prepared cups. Chill until firm, about 2 hours.

Carefully remove the collars before serving. Top each cup with chocolate curls or shavings. Sprinkle the top with a pinch of fleur de sel.

DIY CHOCOLATE CURLS AND SHAVINGS

The first time I saw chocolate curls made on a salt block was in Mark Bitterman's book *Salt Block Cooking*. It opened up a world of new ideas for my confectionery and gave my favorite flourish new flavor. The technique is all about timing; the chocolate-covered salt block needs to be just right temperature for the chocolate to curl properly. The first couple of tries, you may end up with shavings instead of curlicues, but with practice you'll get a feel for what works. No matter what, I urge you to save all your shavings and curls however imperfect *(continued)*

you feel they are. They are all beautiful and tasty. If you don't have a salt block, then you'll find instructions for making curls on a metal baking sheet.

If the chocolate curls seem a bit too daunting, perhaps you'll find chocolate shavings made with a vegetable peeler and a block of chocolate more enjoyable and efficient.

{ INGREDIENT }

9 ounces/250 g semisweet chocolate

Melt the chocolate at 30-second intervals in a microwave at 100% power; stir until smooth. Pour the chocolate onto a 15 x 10-inch/38 x 26 cm cookie sheet and spread evenly with an offset spatula. Or, if you have an 8 x 8-inch/20 x 20 cm salt block, melt half of the chocolate, pour it onto the room-temperature block, and spread it evenly over the surface. Place the coated cookie sheet or salt block in the refrigerator for 5 to 7 minutes, or until the chocolate is firm and has a matte appearance.

Remove the chocolate from the refrigerator and let it stand for 3 to 5 minutes at room temperature. With a small, sharp-edged spatula, starting at 1 edge of the chocolate, begin scraping the chocolate forward in a thin strip. If the chocolate shaves into pieces instead of curling, allow it to stand for a couple of minutes at room temperature and check again by scraping the chocolate forward. The chocolate should curl easily as you run a spatula under it and down the length of the cookie sheet or salt block. Using the salt block will lend a slight salinity to the curls. Place the curls in a small bowl and store them in refrigerator until ready to use.

Chocolate shavings are perhaps easier to make than chocolate curls; you just need a vegetable peeler and a small block or bar of chocolate. Generally, 4 ounces/120 g or larger will work best because you'll have plenty of surface area with which to work. Before you begin, bring the chocolate to room temperature. Use the vegetable peeler to shave flat, thin shavings from the block of chocolate. Let the shavings fall onto a plate and transfer them to the refrigerator until ready for use. Avoid handling the shavings with your fingers for very long because the heat from your hands will melt them.

Giant Red Berry Meringues with Hawaiian Black Lava Salt

I LOVE MAKING THESE RED-MARBLED meringues on Valentine's Day and at Christmastime. I stack them high on a cake stand and they become part of the table decor. Bite into one and you'll find the crisp exterior gives way to a soft, marshmallowy interior. Black lava salt tempers the tartness of the lingonberry jam and gives this dessert a beautiful aesthetic that white salt cannot.

Lingonberry jam is a staple in Scandinavian cuisine. If you can't find it at your grocery store, it can easily be found at the IKEA food market, other international markets, and online. It usually shows up at specialty markets in the United States around November, as it is often used in holiday desserts. Red currant jam or red raspberry jam may be used in this recipe, if you prefer.

{ INGREDIENTS }

Yields 1 dozen meringues

1 cup/200 g granulated sugar

1 cup/120 g confectioners' sugar

6 egg whites, at room temperature

¼ teaspoon cream of tartar

¼ cup plus 2 tablespoons/170 g lingonberry jam

¼ teaspoon liquid red food coloring

Hawaiian black lava salt

Preheat the oven to 170°F/77°C.

Line 2 baking sheets with parchment paper. In a medium bowl, combine the granulated sugar and confectioners' sugar.

Place the egg whites in a spotlessly clean, large mixing bowl and whip them with an electric mixer on high speed until frothy. Stop the mixer and add the cream of tartar. Start the mixer again and beat the egg whites on high speed until they start to thicken. Gradually add the sugar mixture a little at a time.

Beat until the mixture is shiny and holds stiff peaks (this means when you lift the beaters from the mixture, the meringue will stand upright), 5 to 7 minutes.

To make sure the sugar is dissolved, rub a little of the meringue between your thumb and forefinger to see whether any granules of sugar remain. If grainy, continue to beat the meringue until the sugar is completely dissolved.

In a small bowl, stir together the lingonberry jam and red food coloring.

Spoon the meringue onto the prepared cookie sheets in 12 equal mounds (6 per cookie sheet). Use a small spoon to swirl 1½ teaspoons of the lingonberry mixture into the top of each meringue. Sprinkle a pinch of Hawaiian black lava salt over each meringue. Place the cookie sheets, staggered, on the top and bottom oven racks. Bake for 2 hours, rotating the pans halfway through baking. Turn off the oven and let the meringues cool down inside the oven, about 1 hour. When the oven is cool, remove the meringues. They should lift easily from the parchment paper.

Serve the meringues immediately, or store them in an airtight container for up to 3 days.

Always make sure bowls and beaters are spotlessly clean before making meringue. Any trace of grease will keep the egg whites from gaining volume.

Avoid making meringues during humid weather. Humidity causes meringues to weep and become sticky.

Olive Oil Jelly Bonbons with Fleur de Sel

DON'T ASK ME HOW IT HAPPENED, BUT late one night I started obsessing over the idea of an olive oil candy. I was excited and perplexed—a combination that does not result in a restful night's sleep. The next day was spent over the stove, devoted to trial and error, trying to figure out how to make this dream a reality. As we all know, oil and water do not mix. Unless— you emulsify! Now, that may sound like fancy talk to some, but if you've ever made hollandaise sauce or shaken a bottle of vinaigrette, then you've already made an emulsion. I'll elaborate for clarity's sake.

An emulsion is basically two liquids suspended within each other by action of whisking or shaking (or blending, etc.), that otherwise would not naturally combine. Over time, if left to their own devices, the two liquids will separate. To form a more permanent emulsion, you need an emulsifier. An emulsifier is another ingredient introduced to the party that holds the liquids together. It makes sure that, once mixed together, the tiny suspended droplets do not separate back into their two respective liquids. In the end, I found powdered gelatin to be an excellent emulsifier for olive oil and sugar syrup—and with a little elbow grease and a whisk, the olive oil jelly was born. Adventurous eaters will love this! It's less like a sticky gumdrop and more like a soft jelly candy, and the Tahitian vanilla bean lends a beautiful fragrance to it. A dip in semisweet chocolate gives this candy a bonbon makeover, and allows for a sprinkling of fleur de sel before the chocolate sets. Because the chocolate coating is not tempered in this recipe, feel free to use semisweet chocolate chips. If you have a purer form of semisweet chocolate, by all means, use that instead.

There are countless brands of extra-virgin olive oil to choose from, and the flavors are all over the board—fruity, nutty, grassy, spicy, or any combination thereof. I recommend a fruity olive oil that is slightly spicy on the tongue.

{ INGREDIENTS }

Yields twenty 1-inch/2.5 cm-square pieces

Jelly candies

1 tablespoon powdered unflavored gelatin

½ cup/100 g granulated sugar

1 tablespoon corn syrup

½ cup/120 ml extra-virgin olive oil

Seeds of 1 Tahitian vanilla bean

Neutral-tasting cooking spray (optional)

Chocolate coating

6 ounces/170 g semisweet chocolate, evenly chopped

2 tablespoons vegetable shortening

Fleur de sel

MAKE THE JELLY CANDIES

Place ¼ cup/60 ml of water in a small bowl and sprinkle the powdered gelatin over the surface evenly. Let the mixture stand until the gelatin is absorbed.

In an 1¼-quart/1.2 L saucepan, combine the sugar, corn syrup, and 1 tablespoon of water. Place the pan over medium-high heat. Cook, watching constantly, until the mixture just boils—this is important! Don't let the mixture cook too long, or else the candy will not set properly. A good visual cue to look for is when bubbles begin to form around the edge of the pan. When you see this, immediately remove the pan from the heat source. Whisk in the gelatin and stir until it is completely melted. Pour the olive oil in a needle-thin stream into the sugar syrup as you whisk constantly. When all the oil is incorporated, the mixture should be semitranslucent and have a light golden-green color (it could be more golden or greener, depending on the brand of olive oil you use). Whisk in the vanilla bean seeds and immediately pour the mixture into a 4-cup/1 L liquid measure with a pour spout.

Pour the mixture into an ungreased silicone candy mold with twenty 1 x 1-inch/2.5 x 2.5 cm cavities, or pour the mixture into a 9 x 5-inch/23 x 13 cm loaf pan lightly coated with neutral-tasting cooking spray. Transfer the mold to the refrigerator until set and thoroughly chilled, about 1 hour.

Unmold the candies from the silicone mold by running a knife around the top edge of each cavity; push the candies out of the mold from the bottom of each cavity. If using a loaf pan, run a knife between the edge of the candy and the pan, and turn it out onto a cutting board, then cut the candy into 1 x 1-inch/2.5 x 2.5 cm pieces or to another desired size.

MAKE THE CHOCOLATE COATING

Lay out a sheet of waxed paper large enough to hold all the candies in a single layer. Combine the chocolate and vegetable shortening in a small, microwave-safe bowl. Heat at 30-second intervals at 100% power, until the mixture can be stirred smooth. Allow the chocolate to cool slightly before using, about 3 minutes. Use a fork to dip a jelly candy into the chocolate. Lift the candy from the chocolate and tap it on the edge of the bowl to remove the excess. Place the coated jelly on the waxed paper, using a second fork to slide the candy off the first fork. Sprinkle the candy with a few granules of fleur de sel. Repeat with the remaining jelly candies. Allow them to stand until the chocolate is set, about 1 hour.

Store the candies, covered, in the refrigerator.

After making this recipe you'll have a perfectly viable vanilla bean pod for making vanilla pod salt. Chop up the vanilla bean and toast it on a baking sheet in the oven at 350°F/180°C for 5 to 7 minutes. Transfer the pod to a spice grinder or food processor and add 2 to 4 tablespoons of your choice of sea salt. Blend until well combined, about 2 minutes. You may also choose to grind the salt and vanilla together in a mortar and pestle. Use the vanilla salt on shortbread, caramel, cantaloupe slices—whatever you like!

See the "DIY Sea Salts" chapter (page 214) for more information on preparing and storing homemade artisan salts.

Rocky Shore Frozen Terrine with Fleur de Sel

THIS RECIPE WAS INSPIRED BY ROCKY road ice cream, and while it has some obvious differences, such as luscious vanilla ricotta "ice cream" instead of chocolate (more on that later), you'll find many of the usual rocky road mix-ins: chocolate chunks, mini marshmallows, and almonds.

This terrine isn't ice cream in any formal sense of the word, other than being frozen and creamy. There's no labor-intensive custard base to make, and no churning involved. It's simply a mixture of ricotta cheese and whipped cream. I like to make fresh ricotta for this recipe because it's so easy (I solemnly swear!), but store-bought ricotta will work, too. With or without the fresh ricotta, it's one of the easier homemade frozen treats that I rely upon when summer comes and it's too hot or I'm too lackadaisical to turn on the oven.

{ INGREDIENTS }

Yields 12 servings

8 ounces/225 g quality semisweet chocolate, finely and evenly chopped

¼ teaspoon fleur de sel

Unsalted butter, for pan

3 cups/800 g fresh ricotta cheese

1 teaspoon pure vanilla extract

¾ cup/150 g granulated sugar

1½ cups/360 ml heavy whipping cream

1 cup/130 g roasted, salted almonds

1 cup/60 g miniature marshmallows

Cover a baking sheet with parchment paper.

Melt the chocolate in a saucepan over low heat, stirring until smooth. Remove the pan from the heat source and transfer the chocolate to a bowl. Allow the chocolate to cool slightly, until warm (not hot) to the touch. Stir the fleur de sel into the chocolate and pour it onto the parchment paper. Spread it on the parchment sheet to ⅛-inch/3 mm thickness or in a square about 8 x 8 inches/20 x 20 cm. Place the sheet in the refrigerator and chill until the chocolate is solid. Break the chocolate into chunks and reserve for later use in the ricotta mixture.

Lightly grease a 9 x 5-inch/25 x 13 cm loaf pan and line it with plastic wrap or parchment paper, leaving some overhanging on 2 opposite sides.

In a large bowl, beat the ricotta, vanilla, and sugar with an electric mixer until smooth. In a separate bowl, beat the heavy whipping cream until slightly thickened (soft peak consistency). Gently fold the cream into the ricotta mixture. Next fold in the almonds, marshmallows, and reserved chocolate chunks.

Fill the loaf pan with the ricotta mixture. Pick up and drop the pan on a flat work surface 3 or 4 times to pack the mixture down and remove any trapped air bubbles. Cover the loaf pan with plastic wrap and place in the freezer. Freeze until solid, about 4 hours or overnight.

Place the loaf pan upside down on a serving plate or on a chilled pink Himalayan salt block. Soak a dish towel with hot water from the tap and lightly wring dry. Place the towel on top of the loaf pan to warm it slightly and gently pull on the 2 overhanging edges of its liner until the terrine releases in a single piece. Remove the liner. Slice the terrine vertically into 1-inch/2.5 cm-thick pieces to serve. Use a large chef's knife warmed under hot tap water and wiped dry to make an easy job of cutting the terrine slab. Store the terrine, covered in plastic wrap, in the freezer.

HOMEMADE RICOTTA

Store-bought ricotta can be substituted for fresh in the previous frozen terrine recipe, but making your own fresh ricotta cheese at home is easier than you'd think.

When you're buying milk for this recipe, make sure it isn't ultrapasteurized. Milk that has been heated to a high temperature will not yield as much ricotta cheese.

You'll need two batches of ricotta to make Rocky Shore Frozen Terrine, so start at least one day before you need to use the cheese as an ingredient.

{ INGREDIENTS }

Yields 1½ cups/375 g ricotta

8 cups/½ gallon/1.9 L pasteurized whole milk (not ultrapasteurized)

½ cup/120 ml heavy whipping cream

1 teaspoon fine-grain sea salt

¼ cup/60 ml distilled white vinegar

Line a mesh strainer with a double layer of cheesecloth, and place the strainer over a large, nonreactive bowl.

Place the milk, heavy whipping cream, and salt in a large saucepan and heat over medium heat until an instant-read thermometer reaches 175° to 180°F/80° to 85°C, stirring occasionally to prevent the cream from scorching on the bottom of the pan. This will take about 5 minutes. Remove the pan from the heat source and drizzle in the vinegar slowly; stir gently. Stop stirring after all the vinegar has been added. Allow the mixture to stand undisturbed for about 20 minutes. The milk solids will float to the surface, leaving the whey (the watery residue) underneath. Skim the solids from the surface with a slotted spoon and transfer them to the cheesecloth-lined sieve. Discard the whey. Let the ricotta drain for 1 hour, or until most of the liquid has drained away. Store the ricotta in a covered container in the refrigerator for up to 7 days.

Peanut Butter Coca-Cola Cupcakes with Sel Gris

I OFTEN ENJOYED A SIMPLE TREAT OF salty peanuts in Coca-Cola when I was a kid (be sure to read all about it in the Introduction, page 6), and ultimately, this treat was the inspiration for these cupcakes—and this book!

Chocolate cake is made ultralight and fluffy with the addition of carbonated cola. The cake batter will be very thin, but it bakes into a crumb that is tender beyond words. The soft drink brings just the right sweetness and a slight nuance of cola flavor to the cake.

I don't wag my finger at many things, but diet cola is a no-no in this cake. It creates a funky aftertaste and ruins the cake's delicate texture. Be sure to note that natural peanut butter is used in the frosting. It lends flavor without adding more salt or sugar, and makes it possible for the sel gris sprinkled on top to shine. I gave this cupcake many toppings, indeed: sel gris, peanuts, and chocolate jimmies (sprinkles), but of the three I have a firm recommendation for the latter. Chocolate sprinkles can be pure chocolate bliss or waxy and awful. Most of the grocery store brands are subpar. They taste bad. I suggest seeking out pure chocolate sprinkles. The Dutch brand De Ruijter is an excellent choice and can be procured at international markets and online. Or look for sprinkles labeled as "chocolate vermicelli." These are pure chocolate sprinkles that will add real chocolate flavor to your confections.

{ INGREDIENTS }

Yields 12 cupcakes

Coca-Cola cupcakes

1 cup/240 ml Coca-Cola

½ cup/50 g unsweetened cocoa powder

4 tablespoons (½ stick)/60 g unsalted butter, cut into pieces

½ cup plus 2 tablespoons/120 g granulated sugar

¼ cup/60 g firmly packed dark brown sugar

1 cup/120 g all-purpose flour

½ teaspoon plus ⅛ teaspoon baking soda

½ teaspoon fine-grain sea salt

1 large egg

Salted peanut butter frosting

4 cups/480 g confectioners' sugar

8 ounces (2 sticks)/230 g unsalted butter, softened

1 cup/260 g natural creamy peanut butter

¼ teaspoon fine-grain sea salt

3 to 4 tablespoons/40 to 60 ml heavy whipping cream

Chocolate jimmies

Ground salted peanuts

Sel gris for sprinkling

MAKE THE COCA-COLA CUPCAKES

Preheat the oven to 350°F/180°C.

Line 12 wells of a standard cupcake pan with paper liners.

In a small saucepan, heat the Coca-Cola, cocoa powder, and butter over medium heat until the butter is melted. Add the granulated and brown sugars and whisk until dissolved. Remove the mixture from the heat source and let cool for 5 to 7 minutes, or until it stops steaming.

In a large bowl, whisk the flour, baking soda, and salt together.

In a small bowl, whisk the egg until foamy, then whisk into the cooled cocoa mixture. Gently stir the flour mixture into the cocoa mixture.

Divide the batter evenly among the cupcake liners, filling them no more than three-quarters full. Bake the cupcakes for 25 minutes, or until the cakes spring back when pressed in the middle.

Transfer to a cooling rack and allow the cupcakes to cool completely before frosting.

MAKE THE SALTED PEANUT BUTTER FROSTING

Combine the confectioners' sugar, butter, peanut butter, and salt in a large mixing bowl. Beat with an electric mixer on low speed until just combined, then switch to high speed and beat until light and fluffy.

Add the heavy whipping cream, 1 tablespoon at a time, and beat until the mixture is lightened and smooth. Transfer to a piping bag fitted with a ½-inch/1.25 cm plain decorator piping tip or a resealable plastic bag with the corner snipped off. Pipe the frosting onto the cooled cupcakes.

Garnish with jimmies, ground peanuts, and a sprinkling of sel gris.

Fruit Salad
with Thai Chili Salt

IN THAILAND, PRIK KAB KLUA (THAI chili salt) is given as a condiment with fruit. It's a mixture of salt, sugar, and fresh red chiles all ground up together. This holy trinity is the best thing you can put on fresh fruit.

I think we can all agree that fresh fruit is pretty great on its own, but a douse of vanilla-scented syrup makes it superlative. The syrup also makes the fruit slightly sticky, so the Thai chili salt clings to it beautifully.

I use a food processor to make the Thai chili salt, but if you like doing things the old-fashioned way, a mortar and pestle will work just as well.

{ INGREDIENTS }

Yields 8 to 10 servings

Prik kab klua

¼ cup/50 g granulated sugar

2 tablespoons fine-grain sea salt

1 small fresh red chile, seeded and cap removed

Fruit salad

1 cup/200 g granulated sugar

1 tablespoon freshly squeezed lemon juice

Seeds of 1 vanilla bean

(Fruit salad continued)

2 cups/400 g seeded and cubed cantaloupe

2 cups/400 g cubed pineapple

1 cup/100 g blueberries

1 cup/120 g blackberries

1 cup/100 g green seedless grapes

2 kiwifruits (about 150 g), peeled and sliced into rounds

2 cups/400 g strawberries, capped and sliced crosswise

MAKE THE PRIK KAB KLUA

Place the sugar, salt, and chile in the bowl of a food processor. Process until the mixture becomes pale orange and resembles wet sand. Transfer the chili salt to a small serving bowl.

MAKE THE FRUIT SALAD

Combine the sugar with 1 cup/240 ml of water in a small saucepan. Place over medium-high heat and bring to a boil, stirring constantly. When the sugar is completely melted, remove the pan from the heat source. Stir in the lemon juice and vanilla bean seeds. Let the syrup mixture cool completely, about 40 minutes.

Toss the fruit and berries together in a large bowl. Pour the vanilla syrup over the fruit and stir so all the pieces are coated with syrup. Cover the bowl and refrigerate for 1 hour, or until chilled. The fruit can be served from the bowl, or layer the fruit into 4 to 6 individual cups and pour a little vanilla syrup over the fruit in each cup.

Serve the chili salt alongside the fruit salad for sprinkling or dipping.

Pecan Roca with Hawaiian Red Alaea Salt

IF I HAD TO CHOOSE ONLY ONE CANDY to make for the rest of my days (and thank heavens I don't have to), I'd choose this Pecan Roca. Its buttery flavor is similar to that of toffee, but without the rock-hard texture. When you bite into a piece, the candy shatters easily into delicate munchable pieces (in fact, it's a little too easy to eat!). It's studded with pecans throughout and has a topping of melted semisweet chocolate. Granules of Hawaiian red alaea salt sprinkled on top make this candy absolutely irresistible. If you don't have alaea on hand, choose another coarse salt, such as Hawaiian black lava salt or fleur de sel.

I make this every year at Christmastime. It is right at home on a tray for a cookie exchange (although it's not a cookie, I've yet to get a complaint) and a few pieces bagged and tied with festive ribbon makes a darn good stocking stuffer.

While the candy is cooking, the butter may separate a little from the brown sugar mixture, but this is normal. Just let it simmer away without stirring until you remove it from the heat source. I've found that this candy cooks best using a 2-quart/1.9 L nonstick saucepan. Using a larger pot will result in unevenly cooked, separated, or even burned candy.

{ INGREDIENTS }

Yields 36 pieces

Unsalted butter, for baking pan

1½ cups/210 g chopped roasted, salted pecans, divided

1 cup/220 g firmly packed light brown sugar

8 ounces (2 sticks)/230 g unsalted butter

2 cups (12 ounces/340 g) finely chopped bittersweet chocolate

Coarse Hawaiian red alaea salt

Generously butter an 11 x 7-inch/28 x 18 cm baking pan with a lip. Evenly scatter 1 cup/140 g of the chopped pecans in the bottom of the pan.

Place the brown sugar and butter in a small, heavy saucepan and place over medium-high heat. When the butter melts completely, stir until the brown sugar is well incorporated into the butter. Clip a candy thermometer to the side of the pan and bring the mixture to a boil. Reduce the heat to medium or medium-low and boil, without stirring, for 10 to 12 minutes, or until the candy thermometer reads 290°F/140°C.

Remove the mixture from the heat source and immediately pour the hot sugar mixture over the pecans on the baking sheet. Sprinkle the chopped chocolate over the hot candy. Let stand for 2 to 3 minutes, until the chocolate becomes shiny and begin to melt, and then spread them out evenly with an offset spatula. Sprinkle the chocolate with the remaining ½ cup/70 g of toasted pecans and gently press them into the chocolate with the back of the spatula or a spoon. Finish with 1 or 2 pinches of Hawaiian red alaea salt.

Allow the candy to stand at room temperature until it is set and then break it into pieces with a sharp knife. Or you may speed the cooling process by storing it in the refrigerator until the candy is hardened and the chocolate is set.

Store in a container that seals airtight.

This recipe can be made gluten-free by using gluten-free chocolate, such as the Enjoy Life brand.

Coconut Lime Mojito Shooters with Fleur de Sel

IF YOU'RE A FOOD TREND OBSERVER and investigator like me, then you may already know how to make whipped cream from a can of coconut milk. The recipe first gained popularity in 2011 and its favor has endured for good reason. It's simple and delicious. I love using coconut whipped cream in place of dairy whipped cream in recipes, including this one, which is almost like eating Key Lime pie filling from a shot glass.

Sweetened cream of coconut is an ingredient that is used in recipes when an obvious coconut flavor is desired. You can find it with the beverage mixers at the grocery store, as it is often used to make tropical drinks.

{ INGREDIENTS }

Yields 10 servings

1 (15-ounce/440 ml) can full-fat coconut milk

¼ cup/80 g sweetened cream of coconut

1 (14-ounce/425 ml) can sweetened condensed milk

½ cup/120 ml freshly squeezed lime juice (from about 4 medium-size limes)

6 fresh mint leaves

1 tablespoon lime zest

Fleur de sel

Refrigerate the can of coconut milk until well chilled, about 3 hours or overnight. Open the can and scoop out the firm layer of solidified coconut milk on top; place it in a large mixing bowl. Save the coconut water in the bottom of the can for another use (it's terrific in smoothies!).

Add the cream of coconut to the solidified coconut milk. Beat with an electric mixer on high speed until the mixture is fluffy and no lumps remain, 3 to 5 minutes.

In a small bowl, combine the sweetened condensed milk and lime juice. Stir together with a spoon until well incorporated and the mixture is slightly thickened. Fold the lime mixture into the whipped coconut mixture, using a rubber spatula. Mix until no white streaks of the whipped cream remain. Divide the mixture evenly among 10 shot glasses. Refrigerate the shooters until ready to serve.

Just before serving, prepare the mint garnish: Stack the mint leaves on top of one another and roll them up lengthwise into a cigar shape. Using a sharp knife, slice the cigar into thin strips (the French call this method *chiffonade*) and fluff the strips with your fingers so they separate into ribbons. The cut edges of the mint will darken over time, so use the chiffonade as soon as possible. Garnish each shot glass with a pinch of each: mint ribbons, lime zest, and fleur de sel.

Double Chocolate Cream Cheese Brownies with Maldon Flake

I'D NEVER HAD BROWNIE CRAVINGS in the same way I dreamed about a fluffy cake or chewy chocolate chip cookies. Turns out, I was just eating the wrong brownies! Eventually I figured out that using high-quality chocolate in the batter is key (and I mean *key* in italics, caps lock, and with three underscores). I strongly recommend you break out your finest bars and blocks for this very baking endeavor. I'm confident you'll thank me for the advice later (side note: have a tall glass of milk ready to hand).

All at once, these brownies are creamy, nutty, chocolaty, and chewy. And with brittle Maldon flake salt scattered across the ganache topping, they are sure to satisfy every craving. This recipe makes a weighty pan of brownies, so it's a good dessert to take to family gatherings and holiday parties, or anytime lots of people gather together. The origin of this recipe stems from an old *Gourmet* magazine circa 1991 (I still mourn the loss of that periodical). Its version of this brownie was decidedly more adult with an overt coffee flavor. I've made changes to the recipe over the past decade to suit my needs, particularly a greater yield size and a more "potluck friendly" flavor.

Slicing the brownie slab while it is cold will make for neater slices, and you can serve the pieces chilled, if you like, but if patience allows, let them come to room temperature on the countertop. The flavors will be more developed, and you'll be rewarded with a topping that is more cloudlike. You can also better appreciate the crunchable texture of Maldon flake salt.

[INGREDIENTS]

Yields 30 servings

Bittersweet brownie layer

Unsalted butter and flour, for baking pan

8 ounces/230 g bittersweet chocolate, coarsely chopped

6 ounces (1½ sticks)/170 g unsalted butter, cubed

1½ cups/300 g granulated sugar

4 large eggs, at room temperature

1 teaspoon pure vanilla extract

1 cup/120 g all-purpose flour

½ teaspoon fine-grain sea salt

1 cup/130 g walnut pieces

Cream cheese layer

16 ounces/450 g cream cheese, softened

4 tablespoons (½ stick)/60 g unsalted butter, softened

3 cups/360 g confectioners' sugar

Seeds of 1 vanilla bean

Semisweet ganache glaze

6 ounces/170 g semisweet chocolate, finely chopped

2 tablespoons/30 g unsalted butter

½ cup/120 ml heavy whipping cream

1 tablespoon light corn syrup

Maldon flake sea salt

MAKE THE BITTERSWEET BROWNIE LAYER

Preheat the oven to 350°F/180°C.

Butter and flour a 13 x 9-inch/33 x 23 cm baking pan; set aside.

Place the chocolate and butter in a medium saucepan and place the pan over low heat. Stir until the chocolate and butter are melted and well combined. Remove the pan from the heat source and pour the chocolate mixture into a large mixing bowl. Let the mixture stand until it is barely warm to the touch, about 10 minutes.

Stir the sugar into the cooled chocolate mixture with a large wooden spoon. Add the eggs, one at a time, stirring well between each addition. Stir in the vanilla. Add the flour and salt and stir until just combined. Gently fold in the walnuts.

Pour the mixture into the prepared baking pan and smooth evenly with the back of the wooden spoon. Bake for 22 to 25 minutes, or until a toothpick inserted into the center comes out mostly clean with a few moist crumbs clinging to it. Allow the brownies to cool completely in the pan.

MAKE THE CREAM CHEESE LAYER

Combine the cream cheese, butter, and confectioners' sugar in a large mixing bowl. Beat on low speed with an electric mixer until just combined. Increase the speed to high and beat for 3 minutes, or until the mixture lightens in color. Add the vanilla seeds and beat for 1 minute longer.

Spread the frosting evenly over the brownie layer and chill until firm, about 2 hours.

MAKE THE SEMISWEET GANACHE GLAZE

In a small saucepan, combine the chocolate, butter, and heavy whipping cream. Cook over low heat, stirring slowly and constantly with a whisk, until the mixture is smooth, 5 to 7 minutes. Remove the pan from the heat source and stir in the corn syrup. Let the glaze cool to room temperature, about 25 minutes. Pour the glaze over the set cream cheese layer and use an offset spatula to spread the glaze evenly to the corners of the pan.

Chill the brownies for 3 hours, or overnight. Cut the chilled brownie slab with a sharp knife. Garnish each slice with a 2-finger pinch (meaning, pinch the salt between your thumb and 2 fingers) of Maldon salt; add more to taste. The brownies will keep, well covered, in the refrigerator for 5 days.

Watermelon Granita with Hawaiian Black Lava Salt

THE SUMMERS OF MY YOUTH WERE spent beside the ocean. Midseason my family would load up all us kids and a trunkful of pool inflatables, and head for our favorite southern shore. Let me preface this by saying these are some of the fondest memories of my early life, but eight hours in a car with a cousin kicking your seat and adults with raspy voices saying "Don't make me pull over" was more arduous than fun. But on arrival, just seeing the ocean from a parking lot was balm for our weary travel wounds. All was forgiven by the time we changed into our swimsuits, and our first stop was a shaved ice stand that sold only two flavors: lemon and watermelon. This treat was celebratory for two reasons. It began the good part of our trip; and better, it was like an arctic breeze in a disposable cup. This granita reminds me of that shaved ice, and whenever I make it at home it takes me back to those good memories, and a few sunburned ones.

Cold watermelon slices sprinkled with salt have been a mainstay on the southern table in hot summer months, so it was natural for me to add a dash to this granita. Since granita is so icy and meltable, use a sprinkle of coarse salt to finish it. You can use whatever coarse variety you have on hand, but Hawaiian black lava salt gives it a striking "seeded" presentation.

Speaking of seeds, this recipe uses seedless watermelon. It's normal to find white underdeveloped seeds and a scant few black ones in melons labeled "seedless." A few white seeds in the granita mixture won't affect the taste, but remove and discard any black seeds you see when breaking down the melon into manageable chunks.

{ INGREDIENTS }

Yields 6 to 8 servings

7 cups (about 3.25 pounds/1.5 kg) water-melon chunks, seedless or with seeds removed

½ cup/100 g granulated sugar

2 tablespoons freshly squeezed lemon juice

Hawaiian black lava salt

Place the watermelon chunks and sugar in the bowl of an 8-cup/1.9 L) (or larger) food processor or in the pitcher of a blender. Pulse until just combined and then sprinkle the lemon juice over the mixture. Process the mixture in 5-second bursts until smooth. Pour the mixture into a 13 x 9-inch/33 x 23 cm baking dish and freeze for 2 hours, or until icy around the edges. Remove the pan from the freezer and scrape the icy edges to the center of the pan with a fork. When the mixture resembles slushy ice, return it to the freezer and freeze for 2 more hours. Scrape the granita again with a fork into fluffy ice crystals. If the granita is still slushy, freeze again for 1 hour and rescrape. Divide the granita evenly among six glasses. Sprinkle with Hawaiian black lava salt to taste and serve immediately.

This recipe is gluten-free.

Milk Caramel Pops with Smoked Maldon Salt

THESE ARE JUST LIKE THE CHEWY caramel pops you ate as a kid, but better! They're slightly softer and less sticky than their manufactured predecessors, but are firm enough to hold their shape without a wrapper. They are just this side of addictive with a sprinkle of smoked Maldon on top.

When hot sugar syrup and dairy come together it can be a beautiful thing, or it can be a scorched mess. Now, I'm not trying to frighten anyone here, but making caramel can be tricky. A boiling pot of sugar is something that needs your full attention, so forget any intentions to multitask while making this recipe. The key to this recipe's success is to add the cream mixture to the hot sugar syrup in a needle-thin stream while whisking like the devil. Your arm will get a workout, but just consider the calories burned a trade-off for the caramel indulgence.

I suggest cooking these pops to a temperature of 270°F/130°C, which will make them a chewy bite; but a firmer, stickier caramel pop (like those from childhood) can be achieved by cooking the mixture longer to a higher temperature, up to 290°F/140°C.

This caramel sets rather quickly, so it's important to have the lollipop molds prepped with nonstick cooking spray and the sticks resting in the molds before you begin cooking the caramel. One more important thing—sweetened condensed milk is often confused with evaporated milk, so be sure to buy the correct canned milk.

{ INGREDIENTS }

Yields twenty 2-ounce/30 g lollipops

Nonstick cooking spray

1 (14-ounce) can/400 g sweetened condensed milk

2/3 cup/160 g heavy whipping cream

1 cup/320 g light corn syrup

1 tablespoon molasses

1 cup/200 g granulated sugar

1 cup/220 g firmly packed dark brown sugar

4 ounces (1 stick)/110 g unsalted butter, cubed

1 teaspoon pure vanilla extract

1/16 teaspoon fine-grain sea salt

Smoked Maldon flake sea salt

You will need enough lollipop molds to have twenty 2-ounce/30 g cavities. Spray the lollipop molds with the nonstick cooking spray.

Combine the condensed milk and heavy whipping cream in a large glass measure (4 cup/960 ml or larger) or in a bowl with a pour spout. Stir until blended and set aside.

Stir together the light corn syrup, molasses, and granulated and brown sugars in a 4-quart/3.8 L saucepan. The mixture will be thick. Place the pan over high heat and cook, stirring occasionally, until the mixture boils. This will take 7 to 10 minutes.

When the mixture boils, add the butter all at once and stir until melted. Reduce the heat to medium-high and add the condensed milk mixture in a thin stream as you whisk constantly so that the mixture always has a slow boil. Take your time doing this part; adding the cream too fast will cause it to scorch on the bottom of the pan. Insert a candy thermometer into the mixture and let the caramel cook, while you whisk constantly to prevent scorching, until 270°F/130°C is achieved, 10 to 15 minutes.

Once the temperature is achieved, remove the pan from the heat source and stir in the vanilla and salt. Transfer the caramel to a large glass measuring cup (4-cup/960 ml or larger) with a pour spout. Pour the caramel into the prepared candy molds and insert a lollipop stick into each. Turn each stick a half-turn to coat it with the caramel.

Transfer the caramel pops to the refrigerator and let them stand until set, about 1 hour. Remove the lollipops from the molds and sprinkle with flaky sea salt. Package the lollipops in individual cellophane bags, or wrapped in waxed paper.

For block soft caramel, mix the caramel as directed, but heat it until the candy thermometer reads 265°F/130°C. Line a loaf pan with parchment paper so that the piece overhangs the edges of two opposite sides. Pour the caramel into the prepared loaf pan and let stand until set. When the caramel is set, lift it out of the pan with the two edges of parchment overhanging the edges. Store at room temperature in a resealable plastic bag with the air removed. Chop the caramel into pieces as you need it for recipes. Use it for inclusions in brownies, cookies, and pastries.

CHAPTER 3

A DASH OR TWO

It's evident that salty, snacky indulgences get a lot of focus in this chapter, and unapologetically so. Chips and pretzels start showing up as inclusions in all kinds of confections. It's easy and fun to get playful with snack foods, but seeking out the best quality of these is serious business. Whenever possible, choose mindfully made snackables with limited ingredients. My favorite brand of kettle chips has just three ingredients: potatoes, oil, and sea salt. Many food manufacturers are adding sea salt to their goods for health benefits and improved flavor. Look for packages labeled "with sea salt," and taste-test them before you add them to your confectionery, to gauge their salt content. If you can't find these kinds of munchies at your regular grocery store, try pursuing the snack aisle at your local Whole Foods store, or another specialty health-food store. There are other ways to make your own mindful nibbles, such as Homemade Microwave Popcorn (page 149). You can best control the salt content and rest easy that there are no harmful chemicals in your popcorn.

This chapter also holds the recipes most near and dear to my heart. You'll find my grandmother's Bacon Fat Buttermilk Biscuits, which aren't really sweet at all, but they are the best canvas on which to paint any kind of jam, comb honey, and most certainly Chocolate Gravy (page 142).

Roasted Cashew Caramel Cheesecake

WHENEVER I SERVE SLICES OF THIS cheesecake to family and friends, I wait for the question that never, ever gets asked. I anticipate "Where's the crust?" but nary a word uttered. No one notices, and I suppose it's because there's too much crunchy cashew goodness going on up top.

The batter for this cheesecake will fill a 9 x 3-inch/23 x 6 cm round springform pan clear to the top, but do not distress. I've never had one overflow during baking. It will puff up quite a bit above the top of the pan, but after it is removed from the oven it will deflate back down to pan height. I understand the need to feel secure, especially when a pristine oven floor is at stake, so you can put a baking sheet underneath the springform pan during baking if it makes you feel better.

Once this cheesecake is well chilled, I usually level the top. This means cutting off the tall outer edge of the cheesecake with a serrated knife. This step is not necessary, but I like the way the cake looks when the cashews are piled around the outer edge of the cake (I also don't mind the leftover cheesecake scraps on an ice-cream sundae). If you'd rather pile the cashews in the center of the cake, that's fine, too. Plan ahead because this cheesecake needs to chill for several hours, and preferably overnight.

{ INGREDIENTS }

Yields 8 to 10 servings

Cheesecake

White vegetable shortening, for pan

32 ounces/900 g cream cheese, softened

3 cups/690 g ricotta cheese

4 ounces (1 stick)/110 g unsalted butter, softened

1½ cups/300 g granulated sugar

3 tablespoons all-purpose flour

3 tablespoons cornstarch

4 large eggs

2 tablespoons freshly squeezed lemon juice

1 vanilla bean

Roasted caramel cashew topping

½ cup/100 g granulated sugar

½ cup/120 ml heavy whipping cream

1 teaspoon pure vanilla extract

1 cup/190 g salted cashew pieces

MAKE THE CHEESECAKE

Preheat the oven to 325°F/165°C. Grease a 9 x 3-inch/23 x 8 cm round springform pan with white vegetable shortening. Line the sides of the pan with a length of parchment paper that extends 4 inches/10 cm above the top of the pan (this will help hold the cheesecake batter when it puffs up over the pan's edge).

In an electric mixer fitted with the paddle attachment, beat together the cream cheese, ricotta cheese and butter on medium-low speed until creamy and well combined. Beat in the sugar, flour, and cornstarch. Reduce the mixer speed to low and add the eggs, one at a time, beating until well incorporated after each addition. Mix in the lemon juice. Split the vanilla bean pod and scrape out the seeds; add the seeds to the mixture and blend well.

Pour the batter into the prepared pan. This cheesecake will puff during baking, but it will not overflow. Bake for 1 hour 20 minutes, or until the edges are lightly browned and top is dry to the touch (the center 5 inches/12.5 cm of cheesecake will not be set). Allow to cool on a cooling rack for 10 minutes. Carefully run a knife around the edge of pan to loosen; allow to cool on the cooling rack for 1 hour longer. Refrigerate the cheesecake in the pan overnight. Remove the cheesecake from the springform pan and place on a serving platter. Level the puffed top edge of the cheesecake with a serrated knife, if desired.

MAKE THE ROASTED CARAMEL CASHEW TOPPING

Combine the sugar and ¼ cup/60 ml of water in a small saucepan. Cook over medium-high heat until the mixture caramelizes and turns a deep amber color, 15 to 20 minutes. Remove the pan from the heat source and gradually whisk in the heavy whipping cream. The mixture may bubble and sputter with this addition, so be careful! Whisk in the vanilla. Let the mixture cool until barely warm but still pourable, about 15 minutes. Stir the cashews into the caramel mixture. Spoon the caramel-covered cashews around the top edge of the cheesecake, and then drizzle the remaining caramel over the entire cheesecake. Serve chilled. Store leftovers, loosely covered in plastic wrap, in the refrigerator.

Strawberry Balsamic Sorbet

THE KEY TO THE SUCCESS OF THIS sorbet is using good-quality balsamic vinegar. The really good stuff is sweet and fruity and has grape must listed as its first ingredient (*grape must* is wine lingo for grapes that have been processed with skins, seeds, and stems). Look for bottles labeled as "condiment balsamico." These are usually of good quality and priced more affordably than traditional balsamic vinegar, which—no kidding—can cost as much as a fancy stand mixer. Avoid bottles of balsamico that list wine vinegar as the first ingredient. They will be too acidic for this recipe.

The addition of Framboise liqueur to this frozen treat punches up the berry flavor, while the balsamic offers notes of fig and cherry. Serve the sorbet as dessert or between courses as a palate cleanser.

{ INGREDIENTS }

Yields 6 servings

½ cup/120 ml balsamic vinegar

¼ cup/60 ml Framboise liqueur

¼ cup/50 g granulated sugar

1 pound/455 g ripe strawberries, washed and capped

Combine the balsamic vinegar, Framboise liqueur, and sugar in a small saucepan. Bring the mixture to a simmer over medium heat, stirring constantly. Cook until the sugar is melted and the mixture is reduced by half. This will take 5 to 7 minutes.

Place the strawberries in a food processor and blend until smooth. Pass the purée through a mesh sieve placed over a bowl; discard the pulp (if you have a high-powered blender, such as Vitamix brand, you may skip this step). Add the balsamic mixture and stir to combine. Refrigerate the mixture until it is well chilled.

Freeze the sorbet base in an ice-cream maker according to the manufacturer's directions. When the sorbet is thick and smooth, spoon it into individual bowls and serve immediately. Garnish with fleur de sel.

If you're not serving the sorbet immediately, transfer it to an airtight container and store in the freezer for up to 3 days.

Ale and Pretzel Soft Caramels

I DEVELOPED THIS RECIPE EARLY IN my dessert-blogging days after being inspired by some artisan candies I spotted at a local specialty store. Since posting the recipe to my blog in 2010, it's made the rounds on countless blogs and websites, such as FineCooking, TLC, HGTV, and all kinds of craft beer websites. I even had a blog reader send me a newspaper clipping from her local paper with an article about these caramels (which I thought was a real hoot!). It makes me happy that this candy is so well loved. It's sweet and salty, soft and crunchy, hops and malty—what more could you ask for?

I've used all kinds of pretzels to top this recipe—twists, sticks, snaps, and nuggets—but my all-time favorite is salted pretzel rods. I love the way they look when the candy is cut into pieces, and the hefty bite of pretzel seems to balance the sweet, chewy caramel best.

I intended this caramel recipe to be buttery soft (and it is, addictively so), but that means the candies must be wrapped individually in waxed paper squares. Once I left a few pieces on a countertop at room temperature overnight and found flat caramel pancakes the next morning. I salvaged the caramels by scraping them off the counter and rolling them between my palms, but the result was ugly pieces of candy.

This recipe is high yield, making more than six dozen pieces, so it's a good idea to cut all the waxed paper squares while you're waiting for the caramel to chill. This will make the process of wrapping the candies much quicker.

Store these candies in the refrigerator and they'll keep longer, about 3 weeks as opposed to 10 days. Whether refrigerated or not, these caramels should be kept in a container that seals airtight.

{ INGREDIENTS }

Yields 75 caramels

1½ cups/360 ml (12-ounce bottle) brown or pale ale, divided

Unsalted butter, for baking pan

2 cups/400 g granulated sugar

1 cup/220 g firmly packed light brown sugar

8 ounces (2 sticks)/230 g unsalted butter

1 cup/240 ml heavy whipping cream

1 cup/240 ml light corn syrup

¼ teaspoon fine-grain sea salt

1 (6-ounce/170 g) package large pretzel rods with sea salt (about 15 pretzels)

In a small saucepan, bring 1 cup/240 ml of the ale to a simmer over medium heat. Watch the pot carefully, because the carbonated liquid can easily bubble over when heated. Stir the simmering ale if the bubbles raise to the top of the pan, to calm them. Cook, stirring occasionally, until the mixture is reduced and syrupy. This will take about 20 minutes and yield about 1 tablespoon of concentrated ale flavoring. Set aside.

Grease a 13 x 9-inch/33 x 23 cm baking pan with butter and line the bottom with parchment paper so that the paper overhangs on 2 opposite sides. Combine the remaining ½ cup/120 ml of ale, the granulated and brown sugars, and the butter, heavy whipping cream, and corn syrup in a heavy 4- to 5-quart/3.8 to 4.7 L pot. Cook over medium heat, stirring occasionally. The butter will melt and the mixture will begin to boil after 5 to 7 minutes.

Clip a candy thermometer to the side of the pan and continue to cook until the temperature reaches 244°F/117°C; this temperature is known as soft ball stage, and will take about 30 minutes to achieve. If you're working without a thermometer (which I don't recommend, but it *can* be done), you can test the caramel in a bowl of ice water to check the consistency. A spoonful of candy dropped into the water should form a firm but pliable ball.

When the temperature has been reached, stir in the ale reduction and salt, and remove from the heat source. Pour into the prepared pan and carefully lay the pretzel rods on top of the candy. Push them down ever so gently, and be careful not to touch the hot caramel with your fingers. Let the caramel cool for several hours at room temperature, or place in the refrigerator to speed firming. While the caramel cools, cut waxed paper into seventy-five 5 x 5-inch/13 x 13 cm squares and set aside.

To remove the caramel block from the pan, run a knife between the caramel and the pan. Pull the caramel out by the 2 overhanging parchment pieces. Turn the caramel pretzel-side up on a cutting board (if refrigerated, let caramel block warm up a little for easier cutting). Cut the caramel between the pretzel rods and then into 1-inch/2.5 cm pieces and wrap the caramels in the squares of waxed paper.

Use a silicone pan for easy removal.

Cinnamon Toffee Fan Tans

MY MOTHER HAS BEEN MAKING THIS sweet yeast bread recipe since she found it in a newspaper in 1976. It's one of the most versatile sweet dough recipes I've tried, and it can be made into cinnamon rolls, doughnuts, or my personal favorite, these Cinnamon Toffee Fan Tans.

To give this dough the Fan Tan treatment, it goes through several rounds of cutting and stacking before becoming muffin-size squares. When they bake in the cupcake pan, the bottoms become chewy, crusty, and almost caramelized from the brown sugar sandwiched between the layers; the tops of the buns fan out into soft, delicate fronds. The word *fan tan* comes from a Chinese gambling game that means "repeated divisions," and if you've ever made these, then you know how appropriately they are named. The butter toffee topping makes these buns more dessertlike, but we eat them for breakfast or whenever we please.

Yeast is a living thing, and like most living things it can be temperamental. Exposure to oxygen, heat, or humidity can hinder the activity of the yeast. In turn, stale yeast will prevent baked goods from rising. Store unopened yeast in a cool, dry place. I keep mine in the refrigerator, or you can store it in a dark pantry. After opening, store it in the refrigerator in a container that seals airtight. If you suspect your active dry yeast has gone stale, there's an easy way to check it, called proofing. You can read about this method on page 27.

{ INGREDIENTS }

Yields 2 dozen fan tans

Yeast dough

1 cup/240 ml whole milk

½ cup/100 g plus 1 teaspoon granulated sugar, divided

1½ teaspoons fine-grain sea salt

4½ teaspoons (2 [¼-ounce/7 g] packages) active dry yeast

1 cup/240 ml warm water (90° to 110°F/30° to 40°C)

2 large eggs, at room temperature

6 cups/720 g all-purpose flour, sifted, plus more for dusting

4 tablespoons (½ stick)/60 g unsalted butter, melted

Unsalted butter, for rising bowl

Filling

4 ounces (1 stick)/110 g unsalted butter, melted

1 cup/200 g granulated sugar

½ cup/110 g firmly packed light brown sugar

1 tablespoon ground cinnamon

Unsalted butter, for pans

Butterscotch toffee drizzle

2 tablespoons/30 g unsalted butter

½ cup/120 ml sweetened condensed milk (not evaporated)

¼ cup/60 g firmly packed light brown sugar

¹⁄₁₆ teaspoon fine-grain sea salt

½ cup/80 g toffee pieces

MAKE THE YEAST DOUGH

Place the milk, ½ cup/50 g of the sugar, and the salt in a saucepan over medium-high heat. Stir until the sugar melts and a few small bubbles appear at the edges of the pan. Remove from the heat source and let stand at room temperature while you prepare the rest of the recipe.

Dissolve the yeast and the remaining 1 teaspoon of the sugar in the warm water in the bowl of an electric mixer. Stir with the paddle attachment or by hand with a wooden spoon until well blended. Let stand for 10 minutes.

Beat the eggs into the yeast mixture, using the paddle attachment on the STIR setting of the electric mixer. Stir in the cooled milk mixture (it should be lukewarm, about 98°F/35°C), and then turn off the mixer and switch to the dough hook attachment. Turn the mixer on low speed and add the flour a little at a time, mixing until the dough begins to become elastic. Add the melted butter and stir again with the dough hook, then add more flour a little at a time until the dough is even more elastic and pulls away from the sides of the mixer. You may not have to use all the flour. Do not add so much flour that the dough does not stick to your hands—it should be a little sticky. Set a timer and knead with the dough hook or knead with hands on a floured surface for 5 minutes, or until smooth and elastic.

Place the dough in a buttered bowl and turn it over to coat the entire surface. Cover with plastic wrap and let rise in a warm place for 1 hour, or until doubled.

Punch down the dough and turn out onto a lightly floured surface. Knead 3 or 4 times, pat the dough into a ball, and cut into 2 equal pieces. Roll out each piece to a 20 x 12-inch/50 x 30 cm rectangle.

MAKE THE FILLING

Brush the dough rectangles liberally with the melted butter. Mix together the sugar, brown sugar, and cinnamon. Sprinkle each dough piece with half of the cinnamon-sugar mixture.

Cut a dough rectangle into five 12 x 4-inch/30 x 10 cm strips; stack the dough strips. Cut each stack of strips into six 4 x 2-inch/10 x 5 cm rectangles, then cut each in half crosswise to form twelve 2 x 2-inch/5 x 5 cm) stacks. Place each stacked square, cut-side up, into the well of a lightly greased 12-well standard cupcake pan. Cover loosely with plastic wrap and let the buns rise in a draft-free, warm place, 45 minutes to 1 hour, or until the rolls rise about ¾ inch/2 cm above the rim of the pan. Repeat the process with the second dough rectangle.

Preheat the oven to 400°F/200°C. Bake the rolls for 15 to 20 minutes, or until golden. Keep a close eye on them so they don't overbake. Let the rolls cool in the pans for 5 minutes, and then transfer them to a cooling rack.

MAKE THE BUTTERSCOTCH TOFFEE DRIZZLE

In a 1-quart/950 ml saucepan, stir all the butterscotch toffee drizzle ingredients together, except the toffee pieces. Place over medium-high heat until the sugar is melted and the mixture can be stirred smooth with a whisk, 5 to 7 minutes. Let cool until barely warm but still pourable. Drizzle a little of the mixture over each roll, or dip the top of each roll in the sauce. Sprinkle each roll with some of the butterscotch toffee pieces. Store the rolls in an airtight container.

Bacon Fat Buttermilk Biscuits with Chocolate Gravy

IN 2013 I WAS ASKED BY FOOD52, A popular food website, to write an article about a family heirloom recipe. There was only one that hummed through my brain as I read the e-mail request, but I didn't want to share it. If my grandmother's Bacon Fat Buttermilk Biscuit recipe was going on anyone's website, it should be my own, I thought. But ultimately, the desire to share this recipe with an audience larger than my own was greater than my stingy side. I'm so thankful I came to that decision.

In that article, I talked about how my grandmother's buttermilk biscuits sustained my grandfather as he worked in the Tennessee coal mines, and how they were a staple at her table through the Great Depression. How years later she'd bake those same biscuits for her children, then grandchildren—and even her many great-grandchildren. I struggled mightily to articulate the meaningfulness of this sustenance. I felt if I could convey, just a little bit, how these biscuits were—and still are—a beloved part of our family's southern heritage, that would be enough. I could be happy with that.

The story and recipe was picked up by a rather large search engine site, gaining more exposure for this humble recipe than I could have hoped for. There was an outpouring of love, stories, questions, recipes, nostalgia, all directed to my inbox. I learned that coal miners, retired and otherwise, write eloquent e-mails. I learned that we taste with our heart as much as with our tongue. I learned that a simple mixture of flour, fat, and buttermilk could unify a great many people. This was a gift to me, and a lesson.

In this recipe, bacon fat adds a whole new dimension of flavor to these biscuits, a smoky richness. Fat from cured bacon is not sold in stores, so you'll have to render your own. That may sound complicated, but it's not. Just fry bacon on the stovetop as usual, and when the bacon is crisp and all the fat has melted into the pan, pour it into a heatproof jar. The bacon dregs

(if there are any) will collect on the bottom of the jar and the bacon fat above will turn white and solid as it cools. Store the jar in the refrigerator after it cools completely. You'll want the fat to be cold for flaky biscuit making.

A pastry blender will make quick work of cutting the fat into the flour, or you can use a simple hand chopper as I do. My grandmother's method was even more low-tech. She'd rub the fat into the flour with her fingers.

The bacon fat will naturally lend a little saltiness to the biscuits, but not quite enough to realize its full flavor potential. That is remedied with a little fine-grain salt in the biscuit dough.

Chocolate gravy is another family recipe that stems from the Depression era with roots deep in Appalachian culture. Originally it was made with water, but in these prosperous days it is made with milk or cream. It's like a cross between chocolate syrup and chocolate pudding. I've been told my grandmother made it often, but I remember it best on my Aunt Grace's table. She'd put on the biggest breakfast spread, ever.

The best way to enjoy chocolate gravy is poured liberally over a split bacon fat buttermilk biscuit still warm from the oven. Add crumbled bacon on top of chocolate biscuits and gravy if you're that kind of person. I am.

{ INGREDIENTS }

Yields twelve 2-inch/5 cm biscuits and 2 cups/480 ml chocolate gravy

Biscuits

2 cups/240 g all-purpose flour (White Lily preferred), plus more for rolling out

4 teaspoons baking powder

¼ teaspoon baking soda

¾ teaspoon fine-grain sea salt

4 tablespoons bacon fat, cold

1 cup/240 ml buttermilk, chilled, plus up to ¼ cup/60 ml more if needed

Nonstick cooking spray

Chocolate gravy

4 tablespoons unsweetened natural cocoa powder, sifted

2 tablespoons all-purpose flour

1 cup/200 g granulated sugar

1½ cups/360 ml whole milk

4 tablespoons (½ stick)/60 g unsalted butter

1 teaspoon pure vanilla extract

⌒ MAKE THE BISCUITS ⌒

Preheat the oven to 450°F/230°C.

Whisk together the flour, baking powder, baking soda, and salt in a large mixing bowl. Add the fat to the bowl and cut it into the flour mixture with a pastry blender or a fork until pea-size crumbs form. Make a well in the center and pour in the chilled buttermilk. Stir until just combined. The dough should be very sticky; if it isn't, add up to ¼ cup/60 ml more buttermilk until the dough is wet and sticky.

Lay a large piece of waxed paper on a work surface and dust liberally with flour. Turn out the dough onto the floured surface and liberally sprinkle the surface of the dough with more flour. Pat down the dough with your hands, then gently fold the dough onto itself 4 to 6 times, dusting the dough with extra flour as your hands find sticky dough (in other words, don't fiddle with the dough much; no true kneading is required). Dust with more flour if the dough sticks to your hands. Press the dough into a 1-inch/2.5 cm-thick round. Cut out biscuits with a 2-inch/5 cm round cutter. Place the biscuits on a lightly greased baking sheet so that they just touch. Reroll the scraps and cut more biscuits (you should have 12 altogether).

Bake the biscuits until they are golden on top, 15 to 20 minutes. Let them cool on the pan for 5 minutes before turning them out onto a serving plate. Serve them warm with butter and jam or with chocolate gravy.

⌒ MAKE THE CHOCOLATE GRAVY ⌒

In a medium saucepan, whisk together the cocoa powder, flour, and sugar. Pour in the milk and whisk vigorously to combine. Place the pan over medium-high heat and cook until the mixture bubbles. Reduce the heat to medium and stir until the mixture has thickened to a gravy consistency. Remove the pan from the heat source and stir in the butter and vanilla.

Let the gravy cool slightly before transferring it to a gravy boat or serving bowl. Pour or ladle the warm chocolate gravy over the buttermilk biscuits.

Buttered Popcorn Panna Cotta

LONG AGO IN AN ART THEORY CLASS far away, I was introduced to a new word: *gestalt*. It is roughly defined as a work that is greater than (or cannot be described by) the sum of its parts. The first time I made panna cotta and then tasted it, this word came to me and I understood its meaning more clearly than ever. The simple ingredients of cream, sugar, and gelatin could not describe this delicious treat that wobbled ever so slightly before me. Since then I've made it countless times. It's an easy dessert for busy cooks. I've dressed it up with berries and sweet syrups, and I've flavored the cream with whatever citrus oil or spice lingered my pantry. Clearly, I love playing with the recipe and that's how this popcorn panna cotta came to be.

The finished dessert has a mild popcorn flavor, and the popped kernels on top provide a delightful contrast. A drizzle of honey over the popcorn garnish tastes delicious and it anchors the kernels in place, but there's no reason why you couldn't drizzle prepared salted caramel sauce over the garnish instead.

There are many ways to make the unsalted popcorn required for this recipe. You can do it the old-fashioned way in a large pot with oil, or use my Homemade Microwave Popcorn recipe (page 149) for convenience.

{ INGREDIENTS }

Yields 4 servings

8 cups/90 g popped, unsalted popcorn, divided

2 tablespoons/30 g unsalted butter

1 cup/240 ml heavy whipping cream

1 cup/240 ml half-and-half

¼ cup/50 g granulated sugar

½ teaspoon fine-grain sea salt

1½ teaspoons powdered unflavored gelatin

2 tablespoons cold water

4 teaspoons honey

fleur de sel

Place 1 cup/8 g of the popped popcorn in an airtight container. This will be used later to garnish the finished panna cotta.

Pour the remaining popped popcorn into a large bowl, and set aside.

Place the butter, cream, half-and-half, sugar, and salt in a small saucepan. Cook over medium heat until the butter is melted and the sugar is dissolved, about 5 minutes. The mixture should be very hot but not boiling.

Pour the hot cream mixture over the popcorn. The popcorn will wilt and shrink under the hot liquid. Stir the mixture well so that all the popcorn kernels are coated with the cream mixture. Cover the bowl with plastic wrap and place in the refrigerator. Let the popcorn mixture steep for at least 2 hours or overnight.

Remove the steeped popcorn mixture from the refrigerator and stir well to break up the surface if it has solidified. Pour the mixture into a medium saucepan and cook over high heat, stirring often, until hot and steaming but not boiling, about 5 minutes. Remove the mixture from the heat source and let it cool slightly, about 5 minutes. Pour it through a fine sieve placed over a blender pitcher and press the popcorn with the back of a spoon to remove as much of the absorbed cream as possible. Blend on the highest setting until thoroughly blended and slightly frothy, 1 to

2 minutes depending on how powerful your blender is. Let the mixture stand for a few minutes, stirring intermittently, until the froth on top dissipates. The liquid should yield about 1⅓ cups/320 ml of popcorn-flavored cream. If you come up short, add more half-and-half to the mixture to achieve 1⅓ cups/320 ml of liquid.

In a separate small bowl, stir together the powdered gelatin and cold water. Let stand until the gelatin is completely absorbed and forms a solid mass, about 2 minutes. Spoon the gelatin into the hot cream mixture and stir until the gelatin mass is completely dissolved.

Pour about ⅓ cup/80 g of the mixture into each of 4 small dessert cups or ramekins. Chill until set, about 2 hours.

Just before serving, garnish each cup with a few kernels of the reserved popcorn. Use a small spoon to drizzle a little honey over the popcorn garnish. Sprinkle a pinch of fleur de sel over the popcorn garnish.

HOMEMADE MICROWAVE POPCORN

I understand why microwave popcorn is so seductive to snackers everywhere. You can have steaming, seasoned, buttery popcorn at the push of a button. Unfortunately, most manufactured varieties are harboring dark secrets. Read the side panel on the box and you'll find perfluorochemicals (PFCs), synthetic butter, and other undesirable ingredients. The good news is, it's easy to make saintly microwave popcorn at home without all those chemicals. All it takes is a brown paper bag (lunch sack size, about 11 x 3 x 5 inches/27 x 8 x 13 cm), olive oil, unpopped kernels, and—you guessed it—a microwave. One recipe of this popped popcorn with the salt omitted will yield the 8 cups/90 g needed for the Buttered Popcorn Panna Cotta.

(continued)

---{ INGREDIENTS }---

¼ cup/50 g unpopped popcorn kernels

1½ teaspoons olive oil

¼ teaspoon fine-grain sea salt

In a small cup, mix together the unpopped popcorn and oil. Pour the coated corn into a brown paper bag, and sprinkle in the salt. Fold over the top of the bag twice to seal in the ingredients.

Stand the bag upright inside a microwave (do not cook on its side, like manufactured microwaveable popcorn, or scorching may occur). Microwave at 100% power for 2 to 3 minutes, or until the popping subsides. Open the bag carefully to avoid steam, and pour the popped kernels into a serving bowl. Discard any unpopped kernels that may remain in the bottom of the bag.

Peanut Butter and Jelly Long Johns

I NEVER OUTGREW MY LOVE FOR peanut butter and jelly sandwiches, and I have a proclivity for frying them in a skillet with butter, like grilled cheese. This stems from something my mother and grandmother used to do—except instead of peanut butter and jelly, it was simply apple butter fried between two pieces of bread. We knew this invention as a "Lou Vernie," because that's what we do in the South. We name a food after the person who introduced us to it.

I'm told Lou Vernie was a neighbor of my grandmother's during the Great Depression. Times were hard and indulgences were few, but she knew how to make something delicious and sweet with very little. She taught my grandmother this recipe (if you can call it a recipe) and now Lou's treat born of necessity runs through my family like a unifying thread. We all make it, and some of us (ahem) make our own version.

I suppose this seems like a stretch, but Lou is indirectly responsible for this doughnut. If I'd never eaten a Lou Vernie, I would have never fried my peanut butter and jelly sandwiches, and I would have never been inspired to make fried doughnuts with peanut butter and jelly.

Puffy wands of fried sweet dough (called long johns in doughnut lingo) are filled with Concord grape jelly and topped with creamy peanut butter frosting. In lieu of coarse or flaky finishing salt, fine-grain sel gris is used on the freshly piped frosting. It melts away without a trace and creates an invisible layer of salty goodness on top that makes the peanut butter flavor zing!

I use traditional peanut butter, meaning the shelf-stable variety, in the frosting. You can use natural peanut butter if you have it on hand, but I like the extra sweetness that traditional peanut butter brings to the fried dough.

{ INGREDIENTS }

Yields 30 doughnuts

Doughnuts

2¼ teaspoons (1 [¼-ounce/7 g] package) active dry yeast

¼ cup/60 ml warm water (110° to 115°F/40° to 45°C)

1 cup/240 ml warm milk (110° to 115°/40° to 45°C)

4 tablespoons (½ stick)/60 g unsalted butter, softened

¼ cup/50 g granulated sugar

½ teaspoon salt

1 large egg

3½ to 4 cups/420 to 480 g all-purpose flour, plus more for dusting

Unsalted butter, for rising bowl and pan (optional)

Neutral-tasting oil, such as grapeseed oil, for frying

1¾ cups/500 g Concord grape jelly

Frosting

4 ounces (1 stick)/110 g unsalted butter, softened

1 cup/260 g creamy traditional peanut butter

4 cups/480 g confectioners' sugar

⅓ cup/80 ml heavy whipping cream

Sel gris for sprinkling

⌒ MAKE THE DOUGHNUTS ⌒

In the bowl of an electric mixer, dissolve the yeast in the warm water. Add the warm milk, butter, sugar, salt, and egg and 2 cups/240 g of the flour. Beat with the paddle attachment on medium-low speed until smooth. Turn off the mixer and switch out the paddle attachment for the dough hook. Add the flour a little at a time with the mixer running on low speed. When the ingredients come together and form a dough, increase the mixer speed to medium and knead until the dough is elastic, about 5 minutes.

Transfer the dough to a large, greased bowl. Turn it over once to coat the top and cover it with plastic wrap. Let the dough rise in a warm place until doubled in size, about 1 hour.

With a fist, gently punch down the dough. Turn it out onto a lightly floured work surface and roll into a 12 x 8-inch/30 x 20 cm rectangle. Cut the dough into 3 x 1-inch/7.5 x 2.5 cm rectangles. Place the pieces on greased or parchment-lined baking sheets. Cover loosely with plastic wrap and let the doughnuts rise in a warm place until doubled in size, about 30 minutes.

Line a separate baking sheet with paper towels.

Pour the oil into a large pot to a 3- to 4-inch/7.5 to 10 cm depth. Clip a candy thermometer to the side of the pot and place the pot over medium heat. Heat the oil to 325° to 350°F/165° to 180°C. Fry 2 or 3 doughnuts at a time until golden brown on both sides, 2 to 3 minutes. Use a slotted spoon or fry spatula to remove the doughnuts from the oil. Place them on the paper towel–lined baking sheet to drain. Allow the doughnuts to cool completely.

Heat the grape jelly in a microwave-safe dish until just softened and stirrable. Place the jelly in a pastry bag fitted with a plain tip, or use a resealable plastic bag with a corner snipped off.

Hollow out a cavity in each long john, using a long, narrow knife. Hold the cavity open by pinching the doughnut open with your finger and thumb, and place the tip of the pastry bag in the cavity. Squeeze about 1 tablespoon of filling in the center of each doughnut.

MAKE THE FROSTING

In a large bowl, beat the butter and peanut butter until light and fluffy. Slowly beat in half of the confectioners' sugar. Mix in ¼ cup/60 ml of the heavy whipping cream. Beat in the remaining confectioners' sugar. If necessary, add more cream until the frosting reaches a spreading consistency. Cover each long john with frosting, using an offset spatula, or you can transfer the frosting to a piping bag fitted with the Wilton Cake Icer Tip #789 and pipe the frosting—with the ridged side of the tip up—over the entire length of each doughnut, as pictured. Sprinkle the pastries with sel gris just after piping. Store the iced doughnuts in a container that seals airtight.

I'd be remiss if I didn't encourage you to try a Lou Vernie next time you have a fresh jar of apple butter. It's an antirecipe: apple butter (as much as you like) smeared between two pieces of bread and fried in salted butter. And while you're at it, try my peanut butter and jelly version, too. It's simple, delicious, and something to make when homemade doughnuts are out of the question.

TIPS FOR DOUGHNUT SUCCESS

We're all human and mistakes are going to happen in the kitchen, but I find a batch of ruined doughnuts especially sad. Here are a few tips to help you avoid a doughnut disaster.

- If you haven't done so in a while, take a few minutes to calibrate your thermometer; you can find instructions for this on page 29.

- Choose a mild-tasting, pale-colored oil with a high smoke point, such as canola or safflower oil, for frying. Butter and olive oil should not be used for deep frying because they have a strong flavor and low smoke point.

(continued)

- Allow the oil to come to temperature slowly, and do not leave it unattended. It can easily overheat.

- A thermometer is the easiest way to gauge temperature of the oil, but another easy way to test is to drop a pinch of dough in the oil. If it bobs on the surface of the oil and turns golden brown within 2 to 3 minutes, then the temperature is correct. If it sinks to the bottom, the oil is not hot enough and you should wait and test it again after a few minutes have passed.

- Fry two or three doughnuts at a time. Adding too many pieces of dough to the oil will cause the temperature to reduce drastically, and can cause the doughnuts to become heavily saturated with oil.

- Avoid using plastic utensils to scoop the doughnuts from the hot oil. They'll melt and ruin your doughnuts all at once!

- Food particles in used frying oil promotes deterioration, and it can become rancid quickly. I find it's best to dispose of the oil after use—but don't pour it down the sink! When the used oil cools completely, place it in a sealed container and discard it in the trash can.

Sel Gris Pecan Sandies

A ROLL OF SLICE-AND-BAKE COOKIE dough is the best secret you can keep in your freezer. They will save the day when you need a treat for unexpected company, or if your niece needs two dozen cookies for a bake sale—tomorrow. Making this pecan-studded dough is a breeze. My favorite part is cutting the dough into coins. It's the unmessiest kitchen job, ever, so you can don your prettiest apron (the one you don't want to get dirty) and in twenty some-odd minutes, you'll have a plateful of fragrant pecan sandies.

These cookies are everything pecan sandies should be: buttery, crumbly, and chock-full of nutty goodness. I like to garnish each cookie with a pecan half before baking. This makes the cookies a bit heartier and adds extra crunch. Velvet sel gris mixed with sugar makes a delicious coating for these cookies. If you don't have velvet sel gris, regular sel gris or another coarse salt can be ground finely in a spice grinder or a food processor.

The refrigerated dough will keep for three days or store it in the freezer for up to one month.

{ INGREDIENTS }

Yields 40 cookies

Cookies

8 ounces (2 sticks)/230 g unsalted butter, softened

½ cup/100g granulated sugar

¼ teaspoon fine-grain sea salt

1 large egg, beaten

1 teaspoon pure vanilla extract

(cookies continued)

1 cup/120 g pecan pieces, finely ground

2½ cups/300 g all-purpose flour

Salt-sweet coating

⅓ cup/70 g granulated sugar

⅛ teaspoon velvet sel gris

⌒ MAKE THE COOKIES ⌒

In the bowl of an electric mixer fitted with the paddle attachment, mix the butter, sugar, and salt together on low speed.

Add the egg and vanilla, and beat until smooth. Beat in the ground pecans until they are evenly dispersed throughout the mixture.

Add the flour to the mixture in 3 additions, beating each time until just combined. The dough should not be sticky. Turn out the dough onto a work surface and divide into 2 pieces. Place each dough piece on a length of waxed paper and roll it under your palms into a dough log about 2 inches/5 cm thick. Roll the waxed paper around the dough logs and then cover the logs with plastic wrap. Refrigerate until firm, about 3 hours, or freeze for 1 hour.

Preheat the oven to 325°F/165°C. Line 2 baking sheets with parchment paper.

Slice each cookie to 3/8-inch/1 cm thickness and place 2 inches/5 cm on the prepared baking sheets. Bake for 17 to 22 minutes, or until the edges are lightly golden but the centers are still pale. Allow the cookies to cool for 5 minutes before transferring them to a cooling rack to cool completely.

⌒ MAKE THE SALT-SWEET COATING ⌒

Combine the sugar and salt in a small bowl. Dredge each cookie in the mixture. The coating will cling to the buttery cookies.

Store the cookies in a container that seals airtight.

Salt-Baked Pears with Rosemary

BAKING FRUIT IN A SALT CRUST IS ONE of the simplest ways to make it extraordinary. The salt permeates the skins and lightly seasons the flesh just below the peel. During roasting, the centers of the fruit become sweet and soft. It makes for the most divine contrast.

This roasting method is best used with fruits with sturdy skins. Bosc pears and Braeburn apples are both good choices for salt-roasting because they have thick skins and their flesh stands up well during baking. It's important that the skins stay intact; otherwise the fruit will absorb too much salt.

The rosemary in this recipe perfumes the fruit and gives it a delicate pine flavor. It's my favorite herb to use with elegant Bosc pears, but you may also use thyme or lavender sprigs.

{ INGREDIENTS }

Yields 4 servings

10 to 12 fresh rosemary sprigs

1 pound/455 g coarse gray sea salt

4 Bosc pears, firm but ripe, with unbroken, unblemished skins

Preheat the oven to 350°F/180°C.

Space 4 of the rosemary sprigs well apart in the bottom of a 1½-quart/1.4 L baking dish. Place a pear vertically on top of each sprig. Pour the sea salt around the pears until only the tops of the fruit show. Nestle the remaining rosemary sprigs in the salt around the pears.

Bake the pears for 40 to 50 minutes, or until tender. To test the doneness, stick a skewer into the top (exposed) portion of the pear. If it is easily pierced, then the pears are done. If the pears are still firm, bake them for an additional 10 minutes, checking at 5-minute intervals. Allow the pears to cool for 10 minutes in the salt crust.

To excavate the pears, tap on the salt crust with a spoon until it breaks apart. The pears will be very delicate, so don't pull on their tops to remove them. Lift away pieces of the salt crust from around the pears, and then lift the fruit out with a spoon or spatula from the bottom. Transfer the pears to a serving dish or individual dessert plates.

Serve the pears warm or at room temperature.

Try this dish with a side of orange whipped cream, which can be found as the brandy snap filling on page 69.

Chocolate Malt and Fries Ice-Cream Cake

MY HUSBAND'S FAVORITE THING ON earth is a chocolate malt shake, and when I told him about my desire to write a book on salty sweets, he began to talk excitedly about his love of dipping French fries in chocolate malt. It's a love we share. It tastes so good that, in that moment of divine contrasts—sweet and salt, creamy and crunchy, frozen and fried—you almost feel like it's something you invented.

Now, I realize this combination will seem downright bizarre to those who haven't tried it, but next time you have the opportunity with fries and shake in hand, I urge you to take a dip! Especially if the fries are fresh, salty, and crisp, as all good French fries are.

The fries in this recipe are represented with a topping of crispy, fried shoestring potatoes. Add them just before you serve the cake so they are fresh and crunchy. If you are absolutely positively and entirely against the "fries" on top, then omit them and opt for a simple sprinkle of fleur de sel on top of each cake slice.

You can serve this with or without the homemade whipped cream, but a slice doesn't seem complete without a drizzle of chocolate sauce on top.

{ INGREDIENTS }

Yields 8 to 10 servings

2 tablespoons/30 g unsalted butter, melted

1 cup/125 g chocolate wafer cookie crumbs

4 tablespoons granulated sugar, divided

1.75 quart/870 g chocolate ice cream, softened

¾ cup/100 g malted milk powder

¾ cup/40 g fried shoestring potatoes with sea salt

1 cup/240 ml heavy whipping cream

¼ cup/60 ml chocolate syrup

Fleur de sel

Using a pastry brush or paper towel, lightly coat a 7- or 8-inch/18 to 20 cm round springform pan with some of the melted butter. (The cake in the photograph was prepared in a 7-inch/18 cm pan.)

Combine the crushed cookies, 1 tablespoon of the sugar, and the remaining melted butter in a medium bowl. Stir until the wafer crumbs are well coated in the butter. Press the mixture evenly into the bottom of the prepared pan. Transfer the pan to the freezer and freeze for 30 to 45 minutes, or until the crust is solid.

Place the softened ice cream in a large bowl and beat in the malted milk powder, using an electric mixer on medium speed. Pour the mixture over the frozen crust and smooth the top with a rubber spatula.

Freeze the cake for 8 hours, or preferably overnight. Before serving, garnish the top edge of the cake with the shoestring potatoes.

Beat the heavy whipping cream and remaining 3 tablespoons of sugar together in a large bowl with an electric mixer on high speed. When the mixture is thick and fluffy, spoon it onto the top center of the frozen ice-cream cake, or transfer it to a bowl and serve it on the side. Remove the springform collar from the pan and drizzle the entire cake with the chocolate syrup. Sprinkle 1 or 2 pinches of fleur de sel over the chocolate syrup. Serve immediately. Store leftovers, covered in plastic wrap, in the freezer.

Chocolate Chunk Kettle Chip Cookies

YEARS AGO, MY HUSBAND AND I rescued a shelter dog. Before you deem us noble people, you should know we were looking to placate our energetic new puppy with a companion. The picture on the website of forsaken dogs did not convey the strangeness of the dog we met in person. He was old; less canine and more Ernest Borgnine. He stank. He shed. He panted mightily. His short nose was strangely deformed. His skin was so lax he looked like a little man in big pajamas. When I petted his head, he circled two times and lay down before me, chin on the floor between his paws. "He likes you," the lady said, and so my husband wrote a check for the adoption fee.

Once home, I literally scrubbed the ugly right off of him. Turns out, his nose was quite normal looking when it wasn't crusted with whatever it was crusted with. His clean fur was less baggy.

Even though he was primped and perfumed on the outside, he still had some shelter issues to work through on the inside. Some nights he would wake up at one a.m. and I'd take him downstairs so he could check on his food bowl. He needed to know it was still there, and then he'd bark over it for a little while.

Many of these early mornings were noisy and sleepless and boring, so I'd bake. I made whatever was easiest, usually cookies, and I experimented with whatever ingredients inhabited my pantry in those wee hours. The very best of those experiments yielded these cookies. Turns out, crunchy kettle-cooked chips and chocolate chunks in brown sugar cookie batter is a comforting combination, especially when late hours turn into early hours. I often refer to them as midnight snack cookies, because they always hit the spot when I'm restless and craving a nibble before bed.

In this recipe, I reserve some of the chocolate chunks, nuts, and most important, the kettle chips to stud the unbaked cookies. This makes the finished cookie look bakery made and you can best appreciate the crunch and salt of the potato chips. Note: If you are a dog owner, then you probably already know that chocolate is toxic to dogs. While I nibble on these midnight snack cookies, our good boy usually gets a midnight dog biscuit.

{ INGREDIENTS }

Yields 32 cookies

8 ounces (2 sticks)/230 g unsalted butter, softened

¾ cup/150 g granulated sugar

¾ cup/165 g firmly packed light brown sugar

1 teaspoon pure vanilla extract

2 large eggs

2½ cups/300 g all-purpose flour

1 teaspoon baking soda

¼ teaspoon fine-grain sea salt

2 cups/280 g dark chocolate chunks

6 ounces/170 g walnut halves

2 cups/85 g coarsely broken kettle-baked potato chips with sea salt

Preheat the oven to 375°F/190°C.

Cover 2 (or 3) baking sheets with parchment paper or silicone baking mats.

In the bowl of an electric mixer fitted with the paddle attachment, beat the butter and granulated and brown sugars together on medium speed until creamy. If using a handheld electric mixer, beat on low speed until combined and creamy, about 3 minutes. Beat in the vanilla. Beat in the eggs, one at a time, mixing well after each addition. Scrape down the sides of the mixing bowl and mix again briefly.

In a separate medium bowl, whisk together the flour, baking soda, and sea salt. Pour it into the butter mixture and mix on low speed until all the flour is incorporated. Set aside separately about one third of each: chocolate chunks, walnuts, and kettle-cooked chips. Stir in the remaining chocolate chunks, nuts, and kettle chips.

Drop the dough by the heaping tablespoonsful onto the prepared pans, spacing them well apart and placing only 6 dough mounds per pan. Stud the dough with some of the reserved inclusions. Bake for 9 to 11 minutes, or until the edges of the cookies are golden and the centers are still pale. Allow the cookies to cool on the baking sheets for 5 to 7 minutes, or until they are firm enough to transfer to a cooling rack. When cookies are completely cool, store them in a container that seals airtight.

It's better for the cookies to cool on the baking sheets longer, so they are sure to be firmly set; they will tear if they are removed too soon.

CHAPTER 4

WELL-SEASONED

Throughout the previous chapters we've used salt in almost every way imaginable. In the first chapter, it was used as leaven and to round out flavor. In the second chapter, we placed it front and center on desserts for a pop of flavor and as a showy garnish. In the third chapter, we graced desserts with salty pretzels and chips. So, what's left to do? Much!

This chapter has a mix of all kinds of salty sweets, and there's no toeing the line. These recipes go way beyond what's expected as ingredients, including, for example, Kalamata olives or sharp Cheddar. They have savory umami elements that create exciting, complex flavors in desserts.

So, what is umami? Allow me to explain.

Most of us recognize the four basic tastes as sweet, salty, sour, and bitter, but there's a fifth taste called umami. This funny-sounding Japanese word refers to an almost indescribable deliciousness or "mouth-filling" flavor. It is roughly translated as "pleasantly savory" and is actually the taste of glutamate. Glutamate is a natural part of our diet and can be found in all kinds of common foods, such as green tea, olives, mushrooms, and tomatoes. Proteins that have been partially broken down, such as those found in aged cheeses, cured meats, and fermented soy products (miso paste and soy sauce), are especially rich in umami. Many of these umami ingredients are inherently salty, so finding a way to incorporate them into these dessert recipes was a new and exciting challenge for me.

Umami desserts are a relatively new idea in confectionery but it's quickly becoming more appreciated, thanks to pastry chefs and bakeries adding them to their menus. It can be hard to recognize umami when you encounter it, as it is sometimes quite subtle, but like salt it plays an important role making food taste delicious.

You'll find many umami recipes in this chapter, from cupcakes made with white miso paste to red wine–glazed doughnuts. I'm excited for you to try them all!

Lemon Pie with Soda Cracker Crust

FEW OTHER FLAVORS TRANSPORT ME backward in time with such velocity. While I was growing up, my mother made a version of this pie and I was prone to sneak a piece before it was well chilled. I didn't care about neat slices back then and scooping the filling onto my plate with a spoon was the norm. Since then, I've grown a modicum of patience and will allow the pie to firm in the refrigerator, but licking the spatula is something I'm not willing to share.

It's amazing how ordinary soda crackers are transformed into something special with the additions of butter and sugar (and a few minutes in the oven). The crust gives the pie an unexpected flavor that people rave about but can't put a finger on. It is a close approximation of the crust Bill Smith uses on his citrusy Atlantic Beach Pie. (He's the award-winning chef at Crook's Corner in Chapel Hill, North Carolina.) Although he takes no credit for inventing it, he certainly introduced the world to a whole new realm of piecrust possibility. When I first made this pie, my discerning husband scarfed down a piece and then asked, "The crust . . . what is it?" My mother asked what kind of nuts I put into it.

I like to finish the whipped cream topping with exactly one pinch of fleur de sel and a few ribbons of lemon zest, or a homemade salt blend of sel gris and lemon zest (see page 221).

My mother always added a little yellow food coloring to the pie filling and I do, too, but this is optional. Without the food coloring, the filling will be very pale but no less delicious.

Yields 8 servings

Crust

50 saltine soda crackers (about 12½ sheets/160 g)

3 tablespoons granulated sugar

4 ounces (1 stick)/110 g unsalted butter, softened

Filling

1¼ cups/390 g sweetened condensed milk

½ cup/120 ml freshly squeezed lemon juice (from about 4 lemons)

2 drops yellow food coloring (optional)

1½ cups/360 ml heavy whipping cream, divided

2 tablespoons granulated sugar

Lemon zest ribbons, for garnish

Lemon slice, for garnish

Fleur de sel

MAKE THE CRUST

Preheat the oven to 350°F/180°C.

Place the soda crackers in a resealable plastic bag and finely crush them by squeezing them with your hands. Add the sugar and shake the bag to combine. Pour the crumbs into a medium bowl and add the butter. Knead the butter into the cracker crumbs until large clumps of dough are formed. Press the dough into the bottom of a 9-inch/23 cm pie pan and chill for 20 minutes. Bake the crust for 15 to 20 minutes, or until the edges are golden brown. Allow the crust to cool completely.

⟋⟍ MAKE THE FILLING ⟋⟍

Combine the sweetened condensed milk and lemon juice in a large bowl. Stir together until well incorporated and thickened. Stir in the yellow food coloring, if desired. Beat 1 cup/240 ml of the heavy whipping cream to stiff peak consistency with an electric mixer. Gently fold the whipped cream into the lemon mixture, using a rubber spatula. Pour the mixture into the cooled crust.

Beat the remaining ½ cup/120 ml of the cream and the sugar together with an electric mixer until stiff peaks are formed. Top the center of the pie with the whipped cream and garnish with the lemon zest and lemon slice. Sprinkle 1 pinch of fleur de sel on top of the pie.

Store the pie, covered with plastic wrap, in the refrigerator.

Miso Caramel Cupcakes

MISO PASTE IS A TRADITIONAL JAPANESE seasoning that isn't usually used as an ingredient in sweets. You may have tasted it before in miso soup or in other savory dishes. It is inherently salty and rich in umami flavor (read more about umami on page 170). Of the three varieties of miso paste (white, red, and black), white miso (*shiromiso*) is considered the sweetest, so one day I decided to experiment with it as an ingredient in caramel cake and frosting, and the results were stellar! The miso paste gives the confection a new depth of flavor. Even my cupcake-eschewing husband couldn't stop eating them. I consider the ramen hard caramel garnish optional, but it's fun to make and looks pretty on top of the cupcakes, or sitting beside them on a serving platter. Sometimes I make the ramen hard caramel just to snack on because I like how the dry noodles give an interesting texture to the deep amber candy. Consider making it if you have free time on a nonhumid day. Humidity will hinder the hard candy from setting or if it does manage to set, it will become sticky and weep.

You can normally find white miso paste in the refrigerated organic foods section at the grocery store, but if it's not available there, you're certain to find it at international grocery stores.

{ INGREDIENTS }

Yields 15 cupcakes

Miso caramel

1 cup/200 g granulated sugar

4 ounces (1 stick)/110 g unsalted butter, cubed

½ cup/120 ml heavy whipping cream

1 tablespoon white miso paste

Cupcakes

4 ounces (1 stick)/110 g unsalted butter, softened

½ cup/100 g granulated sugar

2 large eggs

1 teaspoon pure vanilla extract

1¾ cups/210 g all-purpose flour

½ teaspoon baking soda

½ teaspoon baking powder

½ cup/130 g miso caramel

½ cup/120 g sour cream

2 tablespoons whole milk

Miso caramel buttercream

8 ounces (2 sticks)/230 g unsalted butter, softened

4 cups/480 g confectioners' sugar

½ cup/130 g miso caramel

Ramen hard caramel

1 (3-ounce/85 g) package dry ramen noodles

1 cup/200 g granulated sugar

½ teaspoon freshly squeezed lemon juice

MAKE THE MISO CARAMEL

Place the sugar in a medium saucepan and set the pan over medium-high heat. Cook until the sugar melts and reaches a deep amber color (on a candy thermometer this is about 338°F/170°C, and no higher than 348°F/176°C). Gently add the butter and stir until melted; the mixture will bubble with this addition. Gradually add the heavy whipping cream in a thin, steady stream while whisking the caramel continuously. The caramel may raise and foam with the addition of cream, so be careful! Whisk the mixture gently until smooth. Remove the pan from the heat source and stir in the white miso paste. Transfer to a bowl and let the miso caramel cool completely before using. This salted caramel sauce will be divided and used in the cake and frosting recipes, and the remaining amount will be drizzled over the finished cupcakes. You may also make it to serve with other desserts. It's delicious on vanilla ice cream!

MAKE THE CUPCAKES

Preheat the oven to 350°F/180°C.

Line 15 wells of a standard cupcake pan with paper liners.

In the bowl of an electric mixer fitted with the paddle attachment, cream together the butter and sugar until light and fluffy. Add the eggs, one at a time, beating well after each addition. Beat in the vanilla. In a separate bowl, whisk together the flour, baking soda, and baking powder; set aside. Stir together the miso caramel, sour cream, and milk in a small bowl. Add the flour mixture and caramel mixture alternately, beginning and ending with the flour. The batter will be thick.

Fill the cupcake liners with ¼-cup/50 g level measures of the batter. Bake for 17 to 22 minutes, or until the cupcakes spring back when pressed in the center. Allow the cupcakes to cool completely on a cooling rack before frosting.

MAKE THE MISO CARAMEL BUTTERCREAM

Cream the butter in the bowl of an electric mixer on medium-high speed. Stop the mixer and add the confectioners' sugar. Beat on low speed until the confectioners' sugar is just incorporated, then increase the mixer speed to medium-high. With the mixer running, add the miso caramel a little at a time. Beat until the buttercream is light and fluffy and the miso caramel is well incorporated. Transfer the buttercream to a piping bag fitted with a fancy tip and pipe onto the cooled cupcakes, or smooth it on with an offset spatula. Drizzle the leftover miso caramel over each frosted cupcake.

MAKE THE RAMEN HARD CARAMEL

Break the block of dry noodles into pieces and scatter them across a parchment or silicone mat–lined baking sheet, 14 x 11 inches/35 x 28 cm or larger. Combine the sugar and lemon juice in a medium saucepan. Stir until the sugar resembles wet sand. Place the pan over medium heat and cook without stirring until the sugar begins to melt around the sides of the pan. Stir the sugar and continue to heat, stirring occasionally, until the sugar is amber. Remove the pan immediately from the heat source and pour it over the dry ramen on the baking sheet. Allow the caramel to cool and set, about 1 hour. Break into shards and use pieces of the caramel to garnish the tops of the cupcakes.

Smoke and Stout Chocolate Torte

THIS CHOCOLATE CAKE WAS INSPIRED by my favorite artisan candy bar made with rich chocolate stout and intense alderwood-smoked salt. After first tasting the candy bar, I couldn't wait to translate those flavors into a dessert of my own. It was like nothing I'd ever tasted before. Alderwood-smoked salt is the star ingredient in this cake, and it has an aggressive aroma, so it can stand toe-to-toe with intense semisweet chocolate in this dessert.

Like any good torte, this one has many layers: two layers of chocolate stout cheesecake mousse and two layers of chocolate stout cake. It's best if you use the same size pans for all of them so they all stack neatly for easy frosting. After stacking the cakes, if you find that the layers are uneven, you can trim the away the excess cake or mousse with a knife before frosting it.

I couldn't resist giving this cake two indulgent toppings. It's covered with salted caramel frosting and chocolate stout ganache overflows the top. Coarse alderwood-smoked salt makes a beautiful garnish on the top edge of the cake. The topaz-colored crystals look like sparkling jewels, and they pack a smoky punch of flavor, so it's best to use them sparingly. In addition to the alderwood-smoked salt, I sprinkle two pinches of fleur de sel over the entire cake before serving.

─{ INGREDIENTS }─

Yields 12 to 15 servings

Stout cheesecake mousse

Unsalted butter or vegetable shortening, for pan

2 tablespoons (2 [¼-ounce/7 g] packages) powdered unflavored gelatin

⅔ cup/160 ml double chocolate stout

16 ounces/450 g cream cheese, softened

12 ounces/340 g semisweet chocolate, melted and cooled

1 (14-ounce/400 ml) can sweetened condensed milk

1 cup/240 ml heavy whipping cream, whipped to stiff peaks

Chocolate stout cake

1 cup/240 ml double chocolate stout

8 ounces (2 sticks)/230 g unsalted butter

¾ cup/100 g unsweetened cocoa powder

2 cups/240 g all-purpose flour

2 cups/400 g granulated sugar

1½ teaspoons baking soda

¾ teaspoon fine-grain alderwood-smoked salt

2 large eggs

½ cup plus 2 tablespoons/150 g sour cream

Caramel frosting

½ cup/100 g granulated sugar

½ cup/120 ml heavy whipping cream

1 teaspoon pure vanilla extract

1 pound (4 sticks)/450 g unsalted butter

½ teaspoon fine-grain sea salt

3 cups/380 g confectioners' sugar

Stout ganache

4 ounces/110 g semisweet chocolate, finely chopped

½ cup/120 ml chocolate stout

2 tablespoons/30 g unsalted butter

¼ cup/80 g dark corn syrup

1 teaspoon pure vanilla extract

───

Coarse alderwood-smoked salt, for garnish

Fleur de sel, for garnish

MAKE THE STOUT CHEESECAKE MOUSSE

Lightly grease two 9 x 2-inch/23 x 5 cm round cake pans with unsalted butter or vegetable short-ening. Line the bottom and sides of the pans with parchment paper. The grease on the pans will hold the parchment paper in place.

Sprinkle the powdered gelatin over the chocolate stout in a small saucepan; let stand for 5 min-utes. Place the pan over low heat and stir until the gelatin dissolves. Remove the pan from the heat source; set aside.

Beat the cream cheese and melted chocolate in the bowl of an electric mixer fitted with the pad-dle attachment until fluffy. Beat in the sweetened condensed milk a little at a time. Scrape down the bowl intermittently and beat until the mixture is consistent and no pockets of cream cheese remain. With the mixer on medium-low speed, beat in the gelatin until combined. Fold in the whipped cream, using a large rubber spatula. Pour the mixture into the prepared pans. Freeze the layers for about 3 hours, or until completely frozen.

Run a knife between the parchment paper and the pans to loosen the cheesecakes from the pan. Turn them out onto a work surface, giving the pans a good whack on the countertop to release them (if that doesn't work, dip the bottom of the pans in hot water for 30 seconds, then try again). Place the 2 cakes on a baking sheet and return them to the freezer. If you're short on freezer space, stack them on a plate with a sheet of parchment paper between the 2 cakes. Wash and dry the cake pans because you'll need them again to bake the cake layers.

MAKE THE CHOCOLATE STOUT CAKE

Preheat the oven to 350°F/180°C. Regrease the two 9 x 2-inch/23 x 5 cm round cake pans and line the bottoms with parchment paper rounds. Combine the stout and butter in a large sauce-pan (6-quart/5.7 L or larger). Sift in the cocoa powder and whisk together until well combined. Remove the pan from the heat source and allow the mixture to cool for 7 to 10 minutes, or until it stops steaming.

Whisk the flour, sugar, baking soda, and salt together in a large bowl to blend.

Whisk the eggs and sour cream into the stout mixture. Pour in the flour mixture and beat with an electric mixer for 3 minutes, or until well combined. Scrape down the sides of the bowl and mix for 1 minute longer. Divide the batter evenly between the 2 prepared pans and bake for 35 to 45 minutes, or until a toothpick inserted into the center comes out clean. Let the cakes cool in the pans.

MAKE THE CARAMEL FROSTING

In a 2-quart/1.9 L saucepan, stir together the granulated sugar and ¼ cup/60 ml of water. Bring the mixture to a boil over medium-high heat. Cook without stirring until the mixture turns deep amber. Remove the pan from the heat source and slowly add the heavy whipping cream in a thin stream while whisking constantly. Be careful with this addition; the mixture will bubble and steam when the cream is introduced. Use a long-handled whisk to avoid a steam burn on your hand. Stir in the vanilla.

Transfer the caramel to a separate bowl and let it cool until it is just barely warm and still pourable.

In the bowl of an electric mixer, beat the butter and salt together until lightened and fluffy. Reduce the speed to low and add the confectioners' sugar. Mix until thoroughly combined. Scrape down the sides of the bowl. With the motor running on low speed, slowly pour in the cooled caramel. Beat on medium-high speed until completely combined, about 2 minutes. Cover the bowl with a damp tea towel so the frosting doesn't dry out as you assemble the cake.

MAKE THE STOUT GANACHE

Combine the chocolate and beer in a small saucepan and heat over medium-high heat until the mixture begins to steam. Remove from the heat source and let stand 2 to 3 minutes; whisk until the chocolate and cream are smooth and well combined. Add the butter and stir until it is melted.

Stir in the corn syrup and vanilla extract. Whisk the mixture again until it is glossy and smooth. Place the mixture in the refrigerator for 5 to 10 minutes, or until the mixture is thick but still pourable. It should be the consistency of thick hot fudge.

ASSEMBLE THE CAKE

Place a chocolate stout cake layer on a serving plate or cake stand. Next, place a cheesecake mousse layer on top of the stout layer and alternate the remaining cake layers so that a mousse layer ends on top. Gently press the layers down so they stick together. Frost the outside of the cake with a thick layer of caramel frosting, using an offset spatula. I ran a pastry comb around the edge of the cake to create a decorative texture after I frosted it, and you can, too, if you have one. Pour the cooled stout ganache over top of the cake and allow it to overflow and run down the sides.

Store the cake, loosely covered, in the refrigerator until ready to serve. Slice the cake while it's cold for the neatest possible slices, and allow the slices to come to room temperature before serving. Store the leftovers, covered, in the refrigerator.

Candied Kalamata Olives

I'VE FOUND THERE ARE USUALLY TWO camps when it comes to olives. You either love them or you don't. If you're an olive enthusiast, and an adventurous eater, then this recipe is for you! These intensely salty and sweet olives are a roller-coaster ride for the taste buds. The first bite will be sweet, followed by a wallop of olive flavor and intense brine.

Deep purple Kalamata olives are savory yet fruity, so they are the best variety for candying. There are countless brands to choose from, and my only advice is to use a pitted Kalamata variety that you enjoy eating. I like seeking out the largest variety I can find (larger olives will take slightly longer to cook than regular ones, of course). Once in the cooking pot vigorously bubbling, they will become translucent and maybe even noisy with little squeaks and hisses. When they're like this, full of sound and fury, that's your cue to scoop them from their amethyst syrup with a slotted spoon and let them cool completely on parchment paper. I usually dredge them in sugar, like candied citrus peel. The added sugar provides a nice crunch and removes the syrupy stickiness. After they've dried for a few hours on a cooling rack, it's easier to use them as inclusions in confections, such as Kalamata Olive Cookie Break (page 191).

{ INGREDIENTS }

Yields about ½ cup/100 g candied olives

1⅓ cups/270 g granulated sugar, divided

½ cup/90 g pitted Kalamata olives, sliced in half lengthwise

Place 1 cup/240 ml of water and 1 cup/100 g of the sugar in a small saucepan. Place the pan over medium heat and heat, stirring, until the sugar is dissolved. Add the olives and increase the heat to medium-high. Cook the olives for 15 to 20 minutes, or until they are slightly translucent and the sugar mixture has slightly thickened and is syrupy.

Transfer the olives to a sheet of parchment paper to cool. Once they are cool, peel them from the parchment and dredge them in the remaining ⅓ cup/70 g of sugar. Let stand at room temperature until they slightly harden on the outside. Store the olives in an airtight container.

Kalamata Olive Cookie Break

IF COOKIES CAN BE CONSIDERED casual, then this cookie is the easiest of the easy-going. You can cut the dough with a cookie cutter to make fancy shapes, but I usually roll it out on a sheet of parchment paper and bake it in one large piece. After it cools slightly, I pull the parchment paper onto the countertop (with the cookie still on it) and that's where it stays all day so we can break off pieces as we care to. The candied olives lend a savory note, and they bring out the nuttiness of the spelt flour.

Spelt is an ancient and highly nutritious grain. It was first harvested in Asia, and later in England over nine thousand years ago. Recently it's come back into fashion because of its rich, nutty flavor and its high content of vitamins and minerals.

Use the preceding recipe for candied olives, or substitute an equal amount of noncandied olives that have been thoroughly drained and left to dry for at least 4 hours on paper towels. Prepared this way, the olive flavor will be more intense in the baked cookie. If you happen to dislike olives, replace them with candied orange peel or candied ginger.

{ INGREDIENTS }

Yields 24 servings

3 cups/300 g spelt flour

½ cup/110 g firmly packed light brown sugar

Zest of 1 lemon

¼ teaspoon fine-grain sea salt

½ cup/100 g Candied Kalamata Olives (page 187)

8 ounces (2 sticks)/230 g unsalted butter, cold, cubed

3 to 4 tablespoons water, ice cold

Maldon sea salt, optional

Preheat the oven to 400°F/200°C.

Place the spelt flour, brown sugar, lemon zest, and sea salt in the bowl of a food processor (6-cup/1.4 L or larger) fitted with a steel blade attachment. Pulse the mixture in short bursts until well combined. Add the candied Kalamata olives and pulse 2 or 3 times in 3-second bursts, or until the olives are well distributed in the flour mixture. Add the cold butter to the bowl and process at 5-second intervals until fine crumbs form. Add the ice-cold water 1 tablespoon at a time with the food processor running at high speed. Stop processing when the mixture forms a ball against a side of the bowl.

Roll out the dough to ½-inch/13 mm thickness between 2 sheets of parchment paper. Remove the top sheet of parchment paper and lightly sprinkle the dough with Maldon sea salt, if using. Transfer the dough, with its remaining parchment sheet, to a large baking pan. Bake for 14 to 16 minutes, or until the cookie is light golden in color and fragrant. Remove the baking pan from the oven and let the cookie cool on the pan for 10 minutes, or until the cookie is cool enough to touch. Break the cookie into smaller pieces.

Store the leftover pieces in a container that seals airtight.

Cashew Caramel Corn

I'LL ADMIT TO BEING A BIT OF A caramel corn snob. If it's not homemade, then I don't want any at all. However, there is one manufactured version that I will concede to eating for nostalgic reasons, and also for the prize at the bottom of the box.

Most homemade caramel corn recipes I've tried tend to be sticky and hard, but not this one. The kernels remain light and airy with a whisper-thin coating of caramel. The popcorn is delicious on its own, but when you add salty cashews to the mix, you've got a truly addictive and munchable snack. It's almost impossible to eat just one or two handfuls, so it's good thing this recipe makes a large quantity—plenty to share (but you don't have to).

This is a family recipe—from my mother's recipe box—and whenever she has the family over for dinner, we all leave with a bag of caramel corn in hand. It's especially good in the fall months because the fragrance of hot caramel seems to perfectly evoke the season, and the miniature specters at your doorstep will appreciate it, too.

The cashews in this recipe can be swapped out for peanuts, almonds, or pecans—whatever nut you find most appealing. You can buy nuts already roasted and salted at the grocery store, but I like to make my own. You can find directions for roasting nuts at home on page 39.

To find the greatest success with homemade caramel corn, make it on a nonhumid day. Humidity will adversely affect the caramel corn: it will make your popcorn sticky and the popped kernels will wilt under moisture.

┤ INGREDIENTS ├

Yields 12 servings

7 quarts/315 g popped, unsalted popcorn

2 cups roasted salted cashews

2 cups/440 g firmly packed light brown sugar

½ cup/160 g light corn syrup

1 teaspoon fine-grain sea salt

8 ounces (2 sticks)/230 g unsalted butter, softened

1 teaspoon pure vanilla extract

½ teaspoon baking soda

Line 2 large baking sheets with parchment paper. Stir the popcorn and cashews together in an extra-large bowl, or divide the mixture between 2 large bowls. Preheat the oven to 250°F/120°C.

Place the brown sugar, corn syrup, salt, and butter in a medium pot and place the pot over medium-high heat. Heat, stirring occasionally, until the butter is melted. When the caramel mixture bubbles, cook it for 5 minutes longer, stirring constantly. Remove the pot from the heat source and stir in the vanilla and baking soda. The mixture will bubble and foam with these additions. Immediately pour the mixture over the popcorn and cashews in the bowl(s). Stir the corn, turning it over to coat it as much as possible. Not every piece will be completely covered, and that's okay.

Bake the caramel-coated corn for 15 minutes, remove the pans from the oven, stir, and place them back in the oven. Bake for 3 more 15-minute intervals, stirring well between bake times as before. After the corn has baked for 1 hour, remove it from the oven and stir it to speed cooling. Break it into pieces. When the corn is completely cool, store it in a container that seals airtight.

You can also divvy the popcorn into treat bags and tightly tie with ribbon for gifts or favors.

Soft Pretzels with Whipped Honey Molasses Butter

I HAVE SO MANY GOOD MEMORIES associated with soft pretzels, and most of them are from when I first learned to drive a car. As a teenager living in a small town, I couldn't wait to get my driver's license. When I passed the exam, my mom generously helped me buy a used car that had a belt problem from the get-go. When I drove it, the squeaky belt announced my arrival a good minute before the car was in view. I should have been humiliated, but you should never underestimate a teenager's desire for freedom; I can testify that it is far greater than a squeaky car belt.

During summer vacation, the noisy car and I would pick up my cousin Amy on the way out of town, and we'd drive forty-five minutes to a mall with a soft pretzel kiosk. We weren't your average shopping-obsessed teenagers. We were there for the pretzels. We'd each purchase one with dipping sauce—although I could have eaten ten—and then we'd sit on a bench in front of the pretzel kiosk and talk about whatever teenaged girls talk about.

These homemade pretzels are so much like the puffy, buttery-soft pretzels from that kiosk—but better. They are heartier, and you can top them with your choice of coarse sea salt and sugar. Also, homemade dipping sauce is 100 times better than any prepackaged pod, especially when it's whipped honey-molasses butter.

There's one step in this recipe that needs special attention. The baking soda bath gives the dough an authentic soft pretzel flavor, and when you drop the twists in the boiling soda water, they'll lay flat on the water's surface and float around, puffing slightly. Fishing them out of the water can prove difficult, and whatever you do, don't pick them up with tongs; your beautiful twisting will be untwisted. The best dipping tool I've found is a large, flat, slotted spatula. Slide the spatula underneath the pretzel so that it lies flat and its entire weight is supported by the head of the spatula. This will help the pretzel keep its shape.

Swedish pearl sugar looks much like pretzel salt, so it feels playful to use it on these pretzels. It also gives them a sweet crunch. Because the sugar is utterly delicious in this recipe, it is worth seeking out. You can find this specialty sugar in the international section at your local grocery store, at international markets, and online. Coarse white sugar or Demerara sugar are suitable substitutes for the Swedish pearl sugar.

{ INGREDIENTS }

Yields 8 to 10 pretzels

Pretzels

1½ cups/360 ml warm water (110° to 115°F/43° to 46°C)

1 tablespoon granulated sugar

2 teaspoons fine-grain sea salt

2¼ teaspoons (1 [¼-ounce/7 g] package) active dry yeast

4½ cups/540 g all-purpose flour

4 tablespoons (½ stick)/60 g unsalted butter, melted

White vegetable shortening or vegetable oil, for rising bowl and work surface

(pretzels continued)

⅔ cup/160 g baking soda

1 large egg yolk

1 cup/180 g Swedish pearl sugar

Coarse Hawaiian black lava salt

Whipped butter

4 ounces (1 stick)/110 g unsalted butter, softened

2 tablespoons wildflower honey

3 tablespoons molasses

MAKE THE PRETZELS

Combine the warm water, granulated sugar, and salt in the bowl of an electric mixer fitted with the dough hook attachment. Stir in the yeast and allow it to stand until bubbly and foamy, about 5 minutes. Add the flour and butter to the mixture and mix on low speed until well combined. Increase the speed to medium and knead until the dough is smooth and elastic, 4 to 5 minutes. The dough should be firm and not sticky.

Grease a large bowl with white vegetable shortening or vegetable oil, and transfer the dough to the bowl. Turn the dough over to coat the entire surface. Cover it with plastic wrap and allow it to rise in a warm place for 1 hour, or until the dough doubles in size.

When the dough is raised, place 2½ quarts/2.4 L of water and the baking soda in a large pot (6½-quart/6.2 L or larger) and bring it to a full boil. Turn out the dough onto a greased work surface and divide into 8 equal pieces.

Cover 2 large baking sheets with parchment paper.

Roll out a piece of dough under your palms into a long rope, about 24 inches/61 cm in length. Position the rope into a U-shape, with the ends pointing away from you. Hold a rope end in each hand and cross them twice about 3 inches/7.5 cm from the tips. Press the ends down into the U-shape at about 4 o'clock and 8 o'clock, allowing about ¼ inch/6 mm of the ends to overhang the bottom of the U. Place the pretzel on the prepared baking sheet and repeat the rolling and twisting process with the remaining dough pieces.

Place the pretzels in the boiling water one at a time, for about 30 seconds. Remove them carefully with a large slotted spatula and return the pretzels to the prepared baking sheets.

Preheat the oven to 450°F/230°C.

Beat together the yolk and water in a small bowl. Coat each pretzel with the mixture, using a pastry brush. Bake for 6 minutes, then generously sprinkle pearl sugar over each pretzel; also sprinkle each pretzel with 1 or 2 pinches of Hawaiian black lava salt. Bake for 6 minutes longer, or until deep brown in color. Let the pretzels cool on the pans for 5 minutes, then transfer them to a cooling rack.

MAKE THE WHIPPED BUTTER

Place the butter in a medium bowl. Add the honey and molasses and beat at high speed with an electric mixer. When the mixture is lightened in color and fluffy, transfer the butter to a small bowl and serve alongside the warm pretzels.

Apple-Stuffed Cheddar Puffs

"APPLE PIE WITHOUT CHEESE IS LIKE A kiss without a squeeze," or so the saying goes. Apple pie served with a slice of sharp Cheddar cheese is common in some parts of the United States, but it might sound strange if you've never tried it. I've always loved the classic combination of fruit and cheese; I'd just never tasted it together in a way that knocked my socks off. I made a mental note to use these flavors in dessert and tucked it away for later. Well, it's later! I've never forgotten that dynamic duo and I love how the two come together so similarly to Cheddar and apple pie in these Apple-Stuffed Cheddar Puffs.

These puffs are made with choux paste (or pâte à choux), the same light pastry batter used to make profiteroles. I learned to make the batter by hand years ago using only a bowl and wooden spoon to incorporate the eggs, but using an elec-tric mixer is much quicker. I often make these in a mixer when I have time constraints or am feel-ing impatient, and you should, too (don't worry, it's not cheating).

In French cuisine, when cheese is added to choux batter, the pastries are referred to as *gougères*, but I simply call them puffs. When choosing Cheddar for these puffs, look for high-quality brands in block form. Preshredded, bagged sharp Cheddar is not ideal for these puffs because they contain stabilizers to help the shreds to hold their shape during transport. Using preshredded cheese will cause the puffs to be too crisp and prove difficult to fill with apples.

I freely admit to being a gilder of lilies. If you are, too, you'll want to make the fried sage leaf garnish. The leaves take seconds to fry and the pop of sage flavor is nice with Cheddar and apple. They make the plated puffs look pretty, too.

{ INGREDIENTS }

Yields 30 filled choux puffs

Pâte à choux

6 tablespoons/90 g unsalted butter

¼ teaspoon fine-grain sea salt

1 tablespoon granulated sugar

1 cup/120 g all-purpose flour

4 large eggs

1 cup/90 g grated sharp Cheddar cheese

Egg wash: 1 large egg beaten with a pinch of fine-grain sea salt

Fried sage leaves

¼ cup/60 ml olive oil for frying

30 fresh sage leaves

Fleur de sel

Apple filling

3 Granny Smith apples (1 pound/450 g), cored and finely diced

1 tablespoon freshly squeezed lemon juice

½ cup/100 g granulated sugar

½ cup/110 g firmly packed light brown sugar

¼ cup/30 g cornstarch

1 teaspoon ground cinnamon

¼ teaspoon freshly grated nutmeg

¼ teaspoon fine-grain sea salt

⌒ MAKE THE PÂTE À CHOUX ⌒

Preheat the oven to 425°F/220°C. Line 2 baking sheets with parchment paper.

Combine ¾ cup/180 ml of water and the butter, salt, and sugar in a 2½-quart/2.4 L saucepan over medium heat. Bring the mixture to a boil and remove from the heat source. Sift in the flour; stir to combine completely.

Return the pan to the heat and cook, stirring constantly, until the batter dries slightly and begins to pull away from the sides of the pan.

Transfer the mixture to a bowl and stir with a wooden spoon for 2 minutes to cool slightly.

Stir 1 of the eggs into the mixture. The batter will appear loose and shiny at first. When the egg is fully incorporated, the batter will look dry and coarse, like mashed potatoes. At this point, add the next egg. Repeat until you have incorporated all 4 eggs. Stir in the grated Cheddar until it is evenly dispersed in the batter.

Transfer the batter to a pastry bag fitted with a large open tip or a resealable plastic bag with the corner snipped off. Pipe the dough into 1 x 1-inch/2.5 x 2.5 cm mounds, spaced 2 inches/5 cm apart, on the prepared baking sheets.

Using a clean finger dipped in hot water, gently press down on any tips that have formed on the top of the choux when piping.

Brush the tops with egg wash.

Bake the choux at 425°F/220°C until well inflated and golden, about 10 minutes. Reduce the temperature to 350°F/180°C and continue to bake until dry, about 20 minutes more. Transfer the choux puffs to a cooling rack and allow them to cool completely.

MAKE THE FRIED SAGE LEAVES

Line a small plate with 2 paper towels. Heat the oil in an 8-inch/20 cm skillet over medium-high heat until hot. Drop 1 sage leaf into the oil to test it. If the leaf sizzles and fries to a crisp within 2 to 3 seconds, it's done—if it doesn't, then allow the pan to heat longer and test again.

Fry the sage leaves 5 at a time for 2 to 3 seconds, or until crispy. Be careful, because the oil will pop as the moisture releases from the leaves. Transfer the crisp leaves to the paper towel–lined plate to drain. Sprinkle with fleur de sel.

⟜ MAKE THE APPLE FILLING ⟝

Toss the apples with the lemon juice and set aside. Combine the granulated and brown sugars, cornstarch, cinnamon, nutmeg, and salt in a saucepan. Stir in 1 cup/240 ml of water. Bring the mixture to a boil over medium-high heat. Boil for 2 minutes, stirring constantly.

Add the apples and bring to a boil again. Reduce the heat to medium-low and simmer until the apples are fork-tender, 10 to 12 minutes. Be careful not to cook the mixture too long or you'll end up with applesauce. Allow the apple filling to cool to just warm or room temperature.

Fill a piping bag fitted with a ¾-inch/2 cm opening with the apple mixture. Discreetly cut a slit in the sides of the cooled Cheddar puffs and fill them with the apple filling. Gently press the slits closed. Pile them high on a serving platter and garnish them with fried sage leaves, if desired.

Serve the filled puffs immediately.

The puffs can be made ahead and stored in an airtight container. Fill within 2 to 3 hours before serving; otherwise, you could end up with soggy puffs.

HOW TO DICE APPLES

You don't have to be a chef to have good knife skills. They're helpful for home cooks and easy to learn. Try this technique I use for chopping apples. It's efficient, and good to know if you have more than one apple to chop (such as the three needed in this recipe!).

Use a large chef's knife to cut off the top and bottom of the apple so that each end has a flat surface. Using a vegetable peeler, peel strips of the skin off from top to bottom, working your way around the apple. After the apple is fully peeled, stand the fruit upright on a work surface and slice off the flesh in four pieces. Get as close to the core as possible when you cut. You'll have two wide pieces and two narrow pieces. Discard the core.

Place the wide pieces cut-side down and slice them in half once. You should now have 6 similarly sized pieces of apple total. Cut a piece in half once, turn to the side, and cut once again. Holding the apple steady at one end, dice the apples into 1-inch/2.5 cm pieces, or finer if dicing apples for Apple-Stuffed Cheddar Puffs.

Overnight Doughnuts with Merlot Glaze

MORE THAN A DOZEN YEARS AGO, MY best friend and I were not only roommates, but also co-workers at an art gallery. I don't know many friendships that survive such togetherness, but however odd it may seem, ours thrived.

The owners of the gallery would often hold special art showings, complete with hors d'oeuvres and wine for the guests who attended. Sometimes these shows ran until midnight, and we'd have to turn around and be back early to open the gallery the next morning. This was a grueling schedule, but we both loved the work and we enjoyed working together, so we made the best of the situation. One morning I came in to find Ann sitting in the break room, doughnut in one hand and a glass of Merlot in the other—the Merlot was a leftover from the previous night's reception. I'm not exactly sure what registered on my face first, amusement or bewilderment, but to this day I tease her about that unusual breakfast. The more

I thought about it, the more it made sense to me. The intense berry and butter notes of Merlot countered by sweet fried dough—it was practically a grape jelly doughnut. I tried the combination and was surprised at how much I loved it, so I decided to make the two into one fabulous doughnut. This recipe is for Ann.

One of the best things about this recipe is that you can make the dough before bed and leave it in the refrigerator overnight. Because the dough is chilled, the doughnuts will take a little longer to rise. My doughnut making usually starts at eight a.m., and I leave the pans of cut doughnuts in a warm place to rise (right next to my oven). In 1½ hours, I can transfer the puffy rounds to a fryer, and that means warm glazed doughnuts by ten a.m.

As in previous recipes using spirits, I suggest using a Merlot you enjoy drinking for the glaze. If you're not a fan of Merlot, substitute your favorite red wine.

{ INGREDIENTS }

Yields 20 doughnuts

2¼ teaspoons (1 [¼-ounce/7 g] package) active dry yeast

1 cup/240 ml warm water (95° to 110°F/35° to 43°C)

3¼ cups/390 g all-purpose flour, divided, plus more for dusting

⅓ cup/70 g granulated sugar

1 teaspoon fine-grain sea salt

1 large egg, beaten

4 tablespoons (½ stick)/60 g unsalted butter, softened

Neutral-tasting oil, such as grapeseed oil, for frying

1½ cups/180 g confectioners' sugar

2 to 3 tablespoons Merlot

Coarse Hawaiian black lava salt

Combine the yeast and warm water in a large bowl. Let the mixture stand until foamy, about 5 minutes. Add 1½ cups/180 g of the flour and the granulated sugar and sea salt. Beat for 2 to 3 minutes with an electric mixer or with a wooden spoon until well combined. Add the egg and butter and the remaining 1¾ cups/210 g of flour. Mix in these additions by hand with a large spoon. When the batter is smooth, cover the bowl with plastic wrap and refrigerate it for at least 2 hours or overnight.

Lightly flour 2 large baking sheets.

Turn out the dough onto a floured work surface. Roll the dough to a ½-inch/1.25 cm thickness. Cut 2½-inch/6.25 cm rounds of dough with a cookie cutter or doughnut cutter. Gently knead the dough scraps together and cut more doughnuts. Place the rounds on the floured pans and allow them to rise, uncovered, in a warm place until puffed, 1 to 2 hours.

Line a large baking sheet with paper towels.

Pour the oil into a large pot to a 3- to 4-inch/8 to 10 cm depth. Clip a deep fry thermometer to the side of the pot and place the pot over medium heat. Heat the oil to 325° to 350°F/165° to 177°C. Fry 2 or 3 doughnuts at a time until golden brown on both sides, 2 to 3 minutes. Use a slotted spoon or fry spatula to remove the doughnuts from the oil. Place them on the paper towel-lined baking sheet to drain. Allow the doughnuts to cool completely.

Whisk together the confectioners' sugar and 2 tablespoons of Merlot in a small bowl. If the mixture is too thick to fall from a spoon in a ribbon, add another tablespoon of Merlot. Dip the doughnuts in the Merlot glaze and allow the excess to drip off. Let each doughnut stand for 1 to 2 minutes before sprinkling with a few grains of coarse Hawaiian black lava salt.

Maple Bacon Pastry Straws

WHEN I BEGAN WRITING ABOUT dessert in 2009, it was just the beginning of what I referred to as "The Bacon Fad." It was omnipresent on food blogs and TV and in every single food periodical I subscribed to. Wherever I looked for new recipes and inspiration, there stood one recurring theme: Bacon is for dessert.

There were bacon lollipops, bacon toffee, and bacon cupcakes. *Candied bacon.* What was becoming of bacon? *Bacon!* Bacon was being hijacked by a fad. Or so I thought.

I approached the idea in my own kitchen with some ambivalence, and perhaps a smirk, but I was curious. I wanted to know just what kind of bacon enthusiasts these bacon enthusiasts were. I love bacon. I love dessert. I just wasn't convinced they belonged together. It seems I'd forgotten all the times I'd eaten Bacon Fat Buttermilk Biscuits with Chocolate Gravy (see page 142).

Here we are more than half a decade later, bacon-topped pastry in hand and one in my very own cookbook. I have to remind myself that behind most every food fad is a grain of delicious truth that sets that fad in motion. I've tried all kinds, but my favorite of these desserts have flavors that hark back to breakfast. These pastry straws are easy to make because they use ready-made puff pastry. They're great for a quick snack or a pregame appetizer, and to me, they taste like the heavenly combination of pancakes with maple syrup and bacon on the side.

{ INGREDIENTS }

Yields 24 straws

1 (17.3-ounce/490 g) package puff pastry (2 sheets)

Flour for dusting

2 tablespoons pure maple syrup

2 tablespoons granulated sugar

1 teaspoon ground cinnamon

1½ cups/180 g confectioners' sugar, sifted

1 to 2 tablespoons whole milk

1 teaspoon pure vanilla extract

6 strips/60 g crisp-cooked maple bacon, crumbled

Allow the frozen puff pastry to thaw completely as directed on the package. This usually takes about 30 minutes at room temperature or overnight in the refrigerator.

Preheat the oven to 400°F/200°C. Line 2 large cookie sheets with parchment paper and set aside.

Lightly dust a work surface with flour and lightly dust a rolling pin. Roll out each puff pastry sheet to a 16 x 12-inch/40 x 30 cm rectangle and cut crosswise into two 12 x 8-inch/30 x 20 cm rectangles.

With a pastry brush, coat a piece of puff pastry with half of the maple syrup. Combine the granulated sugar and cinnamon in a small bowl and sprinkle half of it over the maple syrup. Cover the filled pastry piece with the remaining plain piece of puff pastry and gently roll the 2 pieces together with the rolling pin.

Slice the pastry into long strips and twist, turning the ends in opposite directions. Bake the twists for 15 minutes, or until they are puffed and golden brown. Allow them to cool until they are firm enough to transfer to a cooling rack, about 10 minutes.

For the glaze, combine the confectioners' sugar, 1 tablespoon of milk, and the vanilla in a medium bowl. Stir until smooth. The mixture should be thin enough to fall from the spoon in a ribbon. If it's too thick, add more milk a few drops at a time until the desired consistency is achieved. Drizzle the glaze over the twists and sprinkle with the bacon crumbles. Allow the twists to stand until the glaze sets, about 1 hour.

Repeat the process with the second sheet of puff pastry. Store the twists in a container that seals airtight.

CHAPTER 5

DIY SEA SALTS
Defining the Brine

If you're lucky enough to live in close proximity to a pristine beach and have five to seven days of hot, dry, sunny weather, then you can easily experience firsthand how sea salt is made. A gallon/3.8 L of sea water, sieved to remove sand and shells, can be divided among a few shallow baking pans and left in direct sun to solar-evaporate in your own backyard. As previously stated, this evaporation will take days, sometimes a week or more depending on environmental factors, but eventually crusty salt flakes and crystals will form around the edges of the pans. Soon the completely dry salt can be lifted from the pan with a spatula and kept in a salt cellar or grinder (or both) and used to season food in your kitchen.

If you're like me, and live in a landlocked state that has the kind of summer humidity that will literally curl your hair, making evaporated sea salt is a little more challenging, but it can be done! My own experiment involved toting sea water back home from a beach vacation, the aforementioned sifting and dividing, and then the nervous business of monitoring the sun, possible rain, humidity, morning dew, evening dew, breezes, sudden gusts of wind, the odd thirsty bumblebee, and two curious dogs.

Needless to say, outdoor solar evaporation was a bit too much worry for me, or maybe I just lack the sort of patience that allows a person to truly leave something be (like the watched pot that never boils, watched sea water will not evaporate). So, I took a shortcut. The pans had just begun to crystalize when I transferred them to the oven to finish drying at a low temperature and faster speed. In just a couple of hours, I had two pans that looked like the surface of an alien planet; a landscape so beautiful I found myself at eye level to examine it.

The experience was gratifying (even more so with my oven cheat), and it is something I would recommend to adventurous culinarians and weekend warriors. I mean, making your own sea salt comes with some bragging rights, if you ask me. And I feel that, given the opportunity, few of us are attempting this simple work. It's rewarding to see those small, useful grains magically develop from ordinary sea water—water in which you swam and fought waves for. I felt a sense of irony though, after all the hand-wringing over weather, etcetera, that I could take no credit for making this salt. It had been there all along. I just helped reveal it, and doing so made me feel connected to something larger than myself: the ocean, the land, and its history.

HOW TO REVEAL SALT FROM SEA WATER
(Oven Method)

{ INGREDIENTS }

Yields 3 to 4 ounces/85 to 115 g sea salt

1 gallon/3.8 L unpolluted sea water

Line a large sieve with 4 to 6 layers of cheesecloth and place it over a 6-quart/5.7 L (or larger) bowl. Pour the sea water through the lined sieve.

Rinse the cheesecloth under the tap until it is clean and free of grit, then squeeze it dry. Return the cheesecloth to the sieve and place it over an 8-quart/7.6 L enameled, glass, or ceramic stockpot. Repeat the sifting and rinsing process several times (6 or 7 sieves), until the cheesecloth shows no evidence of sand or grit, and ending with the water in the large bowl.

Rinse the 8-quart/7.6 L stockpot under the tap and dry it thoroughly. Pour the sea water into the pot. Place the pot over medium heat and bring to a simmer. As the water evaporates, the salt will become concentrated and gather at the bottom of the pan in a thick, watery slush. Your kitchen will smell like a stormy sky, or as if a mermaid has taken guest residence in your home.

Stir the mixture occasionally to pull the salt off of the bottom of the pot. After 1½ to 2 hours, when the water has reduced to about one third and you can see a hefty amount of salt under the water, remove the pan from the heat source.

Preheat the oven to 170°F/75°C.

Transfer the watery salt slush to a large glass, ceramic, or stainless baking pan with high sides or divide it between 2 or 3 shallow pans.

Place in the oven and bake for 45 minutes to 1 hour, or perhaps longer, until the pan becomes crusted with salt and all the water is evaporated. The baking time will vary depending on the saturation of the salt, so monitor the pan closely.

Remove the pan from the oven and let it cool completely, about 15 minutes. Harvest the salt, using a spatula or a spoon, and place it in a lidded jar.

It is essential to collect sea water from a clean source. Gather sea water in areas that are known as safe for fishing. Go off the beaten path (or waterway) to seek out the most pristine, unpolluted sources of sea water.

I used stainless-steel pans for finishing the sea salt in the oven, but salt can sometimes pock stainless-steel surfaces. If you're worried about ruining your stainless-steel pans, then opt for glass or ceramic baking pans.

Salt Blends

MAKING YOUR OWN BLENDED SALTS AT HOME IS EASY, AND WILL TRANSFORM pedestrian desserts into something special with very little effort. These homespun salts look beautiful and some of them literally take seconds to put together.

The first rule about making your own artisan salts is that there are no rules, only a few guidelines. The flavor combinations are only limited to your imagination, but there are important tips in this section to help you prepare and store infused salts.

The easiest salt blends to make are those incorporating such dry ingredients as herbs, dehydrated fruit, and citrus zests. Other salt blends that contain wine reductions and wet ingredients need to be dried in the oven or left at room temperature before using. I like using coarse sel gris for most home salt blends. It's slightly damp with sea water, which means the moisture will grab on to the dry elements you add to it. I recommend using a coffee or spice grinder to blend these salts. You could also use a food processor or do it the old-fashioned way with a mortar and pestle.

Fresh Herb Salts

I CAN'T IMAGINE WHAT MY CONFEC-tionery would be without fresh herbs. They lend vibrancy to food, so it makes sense to add them to the element that really makes food pop—salt. In-season herbs can be used to make small batches of blended sea salts.

To take full advantage of their vibrant flavor virtues and because their potency fades over time, these salts should be used within a few days of being made; that's why I suggest making tablespoon-size quantities at a time. These are all primarily used as finishing salts because of their coarse texture and sharp flavor. Using them during baking is not recommended because it diminishes the fresh flavor we seek.

Herbs should be washed thoroughly and patted dry with a soft cloth before adding them as an ingredient. Use the fresh leaves from such plants as rosemary and tarragon and discard the stems. Woody stalks, central veins, and tough spines should be removed from fragrant leaves (such as makrut lime). Use only the most fragrant parts of a plant or fruit. If using fresh flowers, be sure you can positively identify the plants. No guessing! Get unsprayed flowers from a trusted source, such as an organic nursery.

You are by no means limited to the inclusions that follow. They just happen to be my favorites.

Fresh Inclusions: Basil, calendula petals, citrus zests (such as lemon, lime, orange, and yuzu), kaffir lime leaves, lemon balm, mint, rose petals, rosemary, tarragon, thyme.

{ INGREDIENTS }

1 teaspoon fresh herbs/inclusions

1 to 2 tablespoons coarse sel gris

Place the herbs in a spice grinder and pulse in 1 or 2 quick bursts to release the oils and break up large pieces. Pulse again until the herbs are ground to the desired texture. Add the coarse sel gris and pulse again in 3 quick bursts to combine. Pour the salt into a small glass jar, or if using immediately, pour it into a pinch bowl. Use the blended salt as a finishing salt on fresh slices of melon, ice cream, caramel sauce—you name it. Discard unused salt after 2 to 3 days.

Store fresh herb salts in a glass jar. Sel gris contains moisture, as do the fresh inclusions, and they may cause metal tins to rust.

Herb salts can be made finer by processing it longer in the grinder, if desired.

Dried Herb Salts

LUCKY FOR US, DRIED HERBS ARE readily available in the spice section at the grocery store. Unlucky for us, they are not always the best quality. Who knows how long they've been sitting there, and they're usually packaged in clear bottles that will allow light to sap the flavor over time. A good indication of freshness is aroma. But because you can't exactly open the bottle in the grocery aisle and take a sniff, look at what's going on inside the bottle. Viable dried herbs should retain some of their color. Lavender should have hints of blue-purple at their buds, mint should retain some of its green vibrancy, cayenne pepper should be vivid rust-red and not the color of sawdust.

My favorite place to procure dried herbs is at my local herb farm. The herbs are fresher, and thus more pungent and flavorful. They're also mindfully sealed in amber bottles or opaque containers to preserve freshness. I've found that specialty spice shops are also more conscientious about selling fresh, quality products. These kinds of local shops are worth seeking out for the best additions to your flavored salts. You can also try drying your own fresh herbs in the oven. Just line a baking sheet with parchment, spread out the herbs in a single layer, and bake at 200°F/95°C until the herbs are dry and crumbly. The baking time will vary for different herbs, so this process requires a watchful eye to prevent burning.

In general, whole dried buds and leaves should be pulverized in the grinder first before adding the coarse salt. This will ensure your salt doesn't become ground too fine for use as a finishing salt.

Dried inclusions suitable for herb salts extend beyond herbs to spices, seeds, and green tea.

Dried Inclusions: Cacao nibs, citrus zests, dehydrated citrus slices, ground cayenne pepper, ground cinnamon, ground ginger, hazelnuts, lavender buds, matcha green tea powder, mint, rosemary, saffron threads, toasted sesame seeds, vanilla bean seeds.

{ INGREDIENTS }

1½ to 2 teaspoons dried herbs/inclusions
½ cup/100 g coarse sel gris

If using leafy herbs, buds, seeds, or nuts, place them in the grinder before adding the salt and pulse until fine; add the sel gris and pulse in 2 to 3 short bursts, or until well combined. Ground ingredients, such as cinnamon and ginger, will not require more grinding, so they may be added with the salt.

Transfer the dried herb salt to an airtight container. Use as a finishing salt.

Wet and Saturated Salts

THESE SALT BLENDS ARE MADE BY introducing wet ingredients to coarse dry sea salt. Most wet ingredients should be somewhat thick in consistency, like syrupy red wine reductions or chili paste. Aromatic flavorings, such as citrus and peppermint oil, can also be used in blended salts. These oils should be used sparingly, and they should be added to the host salt in drops with a kitchen-dedicated pipette.

The moist sel gris used in the fresh and dried herb salt blends is already somewhat wet and won't work as well for saturated salts, but another drier version of sel gris is available specifically for grinders. This type of salt may be labeled as "grinder" salt, because it can also be used in containers with metal parts that are sensitive to moisture and likely to rust. Sel gris is just one type of dry sea salt you can use; other varieties may be used and are easily found at your local grocery store, but they may lack the underlying mineral flavor that sel gris has. These drier selections will be more prone to soak up all the flavor and moisture of the wet ingredients without causing the salt to break down and melt away.

Some of my favorite wet salts are made using reductions. In cooking, reduction is a process of thickening and intensifying a liquid. This is usually done by placing the liquid in a saucepan and allowing it to simmer until much of the water is evaporated. A good ratio to follow for making reductions for salt is to reduce 1 cup/240 ml of liquid in a saucepan over medium to medium-high heat until 1 tablespoon of concentrated liquid is achieved. Reducing liquid on the stovetop requires some babysitting because the concentrated liquid can scorch easily, so keep a sharp eye on it.

Making these infusions will take a little more preparation than whizzing a few ingredients in a spice grinder and the quantity of the inclusions will vary between ingredients. Following are guidelines to adding wet ingredients to sea salts.

Wet Inclusions: Balsamic vinegar reduction, chili sauce (such as sriracha), molasses, port wine reduction, pure cinnamon oil, pure lemon oil, pure lime oil, red wine reduction, stout and ale reductions.

{ INGREDIENTS }

¾ cup/150 g dry coarse sea salt

1 teaspoon to 1 tablespoon wet ingredients, or 2 to 4 drops flavoring oil

Pour the salt into a large bowl and add the desired amount of wet ingredient. Start with the smallest recommended amount and increase the amount a little at a time to taste. Transfer the salt to a grinder or food processor if you wish to grind the salt to a finer texture; otherwise, transfer the salt to a parchment-lined baking sheet and spread it in an even layer. Allow the salt to dry at room temperature for 2 days, or cure it in the oven at 170°F/80°C for 2 hours, stirring occasionally. When the salt is dry, transfer it to a glass jar with an airtight lid. The salt may become solid in the jar over time. If this happens, break it up with a fork and pulse it 2 or 3 times in a spice grinder or food processor.

online resources and suppliers

BAKER'S JOY:
Flour-based baking sprays.
www.bakersjoy.com

ENJOY LIFE:
Gluten- and allergy-free
chocolate baking chips and bars.
www.enjoylifefoods.com

FAIR TRADE PRODUCTS:
Responsibly sourced chocolate,
coffee, and spices.
www.fairtradeusa.org

FRONTIER SPICES:
Fair Trade–certified spices.
www.frontiercoop.com

GUITTARD CHOCOLATE:
Fair Trade–certified quality chocolate.
www.guittard.com

JACK DANIEL'S TENNESSEE WHISKEY:
www.jackdaniels.com

LARS' OWN SWEDISH PEARL SUGAR:
www.larsown.com

MAEDA-EN MATCHA GREEN TEA:
www.maeda-en.com

MALDON:
www.maldonsalt.co.uk

THE MEADOW:
Gourmet salt and salt blocks.
www.atthemeadow.com

WECK CANNING JARS:
www.weckjars.com

WHITE LILY FLOUR:
www.whitelily.com

WILD TURKEY KENTUCKY BOURBON:
www.wildturkeybourbon.com

index

Note: Page references in *italics* indicate photographs.